Moose

Ron Potter

Moose
Copyright © 2020 by Ron Potter

All rights reserved. No part of this publication may be reproduced, distributed, or transmitted in any form or by any means, including photocopying, recording, or other electronic or mechanical methods, without the prior written permission of the author, except in the case of brief quotations embodied in critical reviews and certain other non-commercial uses permitted by copyright law.

Tellwell Talent
www.tellwell.ca

ISBN
978-0-2288-2659-0 (Hardcover)
978-0-2288-2658-3 (Paperback)
978-0-2288-2660-6 (eBook)

Okay, so this is how it works. You exist now, there is no other time. You think that your life is proceeding from A–Z with all points in between. Life is birth, childhood, puberty, adulthood, middle age, old age, death. Right? This is what you believe. But it is not so. You exist now and only ever now. You change your probable pasts as you change your potential futures from your current moment of existence. And this moment is eternal. You create both the past and the future at the same time, like you exist between two mirrors, each reflecting all versions of you and your choices both ways.

So, I create a past and a future from this point in my life. And I will assign you to be in my past and my future in roles that I choose, and everyone else will be actors on a stage in a drama that I am writing and directing.

Do you think that robs you of free will? Free will is a myth. We are all playing roles written for us by those around us. So I am someone else's actor at the same time that I am my own choice of preference. This is where we sync up. Universes are formed by this synchronization.

And as I change my preferences, I sync up others who share the same ideas and beliefs, i.e. preferences. The possible worlds are endless, as are the potential iterations of ourselves. Madness, mayhem, peace, love, creativity, prosperity, slavish boredom, pain, rejection, hatred, murder, love and union, on and on the possibilities run.

And by the way, we never end. When we experience death, we don't know it. Awareness is continuous. We continue to know each other in all the other probable realities. We never miss a beat. That is why grief is such a waste of time. It only exists here. I never believed in it. We all continue, we never end, not to ourselves and not to each other.

And this is where madness becomes apparent. Not because I can think these thoughts. They are quite common. Everyone thinks them at one time or another. But I live these thoughts. It's not like the Butterfly Effect or Slaughterhouse Five. I can't literally go back and forth in time. But figuratively I can, in my imagination. And when I move my imagination around it alters my now, imperceptibly, but I know that I change when I tell a story with a new interpretation. I start with the old story and imagine it just a little differently than I remembered it. The trick is that I need to believe the new story. And with practice that becomes easier.

And it helps to tell a different story about the past and the future. Oh yes, you have already written your future. It is a fact that the guy who fears a heart attack will have shitty eating habits. The woman who envisions a great retirement already has her funds in place. Those are oversimplified examples, but we are living our futures.

I can reimagine my future and change myself in the now. I do it all the time. But of course, once my beliefs have changed I am no longer aware of the old story, because now that I believe the new one I am living it.

There is just a sliver of a moment, like a slice of a razor, where I can perceive the change. It takes a great deal of energy to feel that shift. I fast for days drinking only water, sleep outside, walk through a marsh—bare feet in the muck and algae, reeds ten feet tall, dragonflies and red-winged blackbirds around me. I'll stand in the quiet for hours, losing my grip. My life story, my fears, my joys, my today and my tomorrow become air around me that I breathe. And then I dredge up a memory, or I daydream a future. I see myself as I knew myself, but the image is thin and I change the event to a new interpretation and I watch it like a TV show. My new self appears, new posture, new eyes, and when he looks at me, that is the moment, that slice of the razor. Then he is gone and I am him. And I am barely aware I was ever anyone else.

So why not start with the future, why not start with my death? As I've said, we all die constantly and it's just a shift of focus. And from where I sit now, from this focused point of attention, there is an end and I am fashioning it with my thoughts and imagination. With my story.

I am old, ninety years old, with a backpack and jeans and old hiking boots, a thick shirt and a Lopi wool sweater knitted by my mother-in-law seventy years ago. I know, that seems impossible. But I have kept it, repaired it numerous times, and wear it as a talisman. As I write this I am in my sixties and it has been forty years since she gave it to me. Actually, she knitted it for my father but he gave it to me. Lopi is an Icelandic wool which is not spun and keeps you incredibly warm, even when it gets wet. As I write this I have it in my hands. The texture is oily and it smells of wood smoke and fresh air.

But here in the bush at the time of my dying it is keeping my old bones warm. I have been walking for about three days on a trail northeast of Belleville, Ontario that I have known since I was a kid. My grandmother on my mother's side was the first one to bring me here. A red-haired daughter of French and Irish immigrants, she was raised on this rocky land by a couple who believed in their blessings, a strong Catholic family whose pride was bolstered by booze and poverty.

She walked me and my cousins down this very path, between tall hardwood trees with sparse grass and the smells of decay. The trees sang with the wind. Farther back was an old log cabin where she was raised. Our families used it for summer vacations. As young adults we used it for wild drug party weekends. My friends and I would do acid, fill our wineskins with Harveys Bristol Cream and cross-country ski down this path and others that traverse the slow hills and bush trails of the area.

I walked past the cabin a while ago. It had been closed up for the season.

It is October and the bush is vivid with colours, the dried rattle of leaves and the clear marshes filling. My old farmer friend Keith always said it would never snow until the marshes were full. It has been raining pretty steadily since I arrived. I drove my truck to the old gravel pit, signed the ownership and left it on the dash with the keys in plain sight. And a note:

Moose

> *Please take this truck. I won't be needing it. Please do not reveal where or how you found it.*

I watched as an old guy, not quite my age, stopped his old truck and got out, walked around my truck and looked inside. He opened the door and sat in to read the note. I could see his bemused look, and then a hint of . . . what? Sadness maybe, a firm lip, a stiff jaw. He reminded me of my father. Guys like him are rare these days.

And my truck is an antique. Now, as I write this it's new, a 2017 Tacoma. But as he sits in it, it's almost forty years later and the truck's still in mint condition. I babied it all those years in memory of my wife who drove it more than anyone. And this man in his overalls and his weathered cap recognizes this as he takes the keys, locks the cab and gets into his own truck to drive away. I can see his face, a kind face of the like seen often in old British TV shows. A George Gently kind of face, or Inspector Lewis, or Lord Peter Wimsey, men who had seen too much but were still kind and able to think deeply. I don't suspect he knew I was watching. And I wasn't. In fact, I was miles away on my journey into the bush. It is I who am watching from a vantage forty years earlier, pen in hand.

The air is cold and wet but I am warm. I recall camping when I was newly married and in my born-again Christian phase, me and my friend Boyd, his son-in-law Wayne and my young church friend Heather's boyfriend Matt. He would later impregnate my young friend in a born-again church scandal that would result in our providing shelter for the girl and the unborn child. Her father had gone nuts and wanted her to have an abortion she clearly did not want. My wife, that bastion of courage and fearless righteousness, that mind of colour and body electric, told that father he might never have another granddaughter from that daughter of his. That he should accept his daughter's will and take her in and protect and love her. Which, to his credit, he did. Even if he was an asshole, he did one thing right.

Abortions, tearing of a soul from life. And do I want to recall the abortion that had left me childless, that left an empty space in my marriage for a child, for the future to be born into? No, I don't. I was not there. I am not a part of that story so I am not telling it. Fabrications are inauthentic and do not belong in this book. I adopted a daughter, the second descendant of a sperm donor and a polio casualty. She was bred from the type of minds that seek grounding, of the type of lives that lack adhesion to societal norms. But still, that adoption and the eventual grandson that came changed me. Before that I was all bravado, all risk and fight. But because of hard times that never ended, I became centred in myself. I came to know who I was. My shoulders became granite, my heart living moss, my blood a stream of beings giving life. I am like that as I watch myself now, with this pain in my gut, slowly growing and taking my place on my ancestors' ground, rock and cedar rail fences and paths a century old and I know, I have always known, I will die here.

And so now I have created him, my dying self, and I myself am being created by him as he recalls his past. There is no fixed point and I am recalling as he is recalling, and I feel the change in myself, the first transformation.

I see myself a boy in Grade 1 in a red brick school in my hometown. I draw a dog in class. My teacher brings it to me, Miss Tamblyn, young and pretty, barely twenty herself. I am not used to kind words. Adults usually speak to me in fury or frustration.

"Ronnie, did you draw this?" she asks.

A shy nod from me.

"It's very good. You should take it home to show your father and mother. You are good at drawing."

I smile, thinking how wonderful it will be. It's good enough to be proud of.

On the way home a boy, Willie, stops me at the entrance to our yard and starts a fight. I push him and wrestle him down. I hold him down and turn and see my father watching from the steps. Willie doesn't see him.

"Do you give, Willie?" I yell loud enough.

He answers yes but then jumps up and at me again. And I put him back down. And I yell at him to give and he does and then I pin him again. I hear my father's voice call. Willie does too and gets up and runs.

I go to my dad at the porch door. "Why did you keep letting him get up?" he asks.

"Because he gave."

"Next time don't let him up."

At supper I remember the drawing. I show it to them. They both smile with casual interest. "That's good, son." I feel my six-year-old heart cringe. I thought it was better than that. My teacher thought it was better than that.

The thought seems to continue, like a strand of gum being pulled, and I cannot stop it. One scene morphs into the next like a dream.

I am in Grade 6 and a boy has made a weapon out of a bobby pin. He pushes it against you and it snaps against your leg, hurting. I see him doing it to other kids. He does it to me. I don't see him coming but feel a sharp prick through my clothes. I turn abruptly and he laughs in my face. "What ya goin' to do, Potter?"

"Do it again and I'll slap you down." He is a weak kid, small and frail and I don't want to hit him but I also don't think he should be hurting me. His Grade 8 tough-guy friend is standing with him.

"I'm thinking you should shut up, Potter," the Grade 8 says and punches me in the face. His name is Couvier and I have never been punched in the face before. I feel the blood rush from my toes to my face.

"You're a big suck, Potter, a big fucking suck."

I am boiling anger out my pores. Behind the ball diamond, with McMahon the teacher right there umpiring the game, I walk up to the bully. He's got six inches on me.

"That wasn't fair. You hit me without warning."

He steps out from the crowd of his friends and stands straight-backed with his head tilted to the right. "What you going to do about it?"

I rush and grab his coat and pull it over his head and start throwing punches into his face. He struggles to free himself but I keep the fists flailing, again and again until McMahon comes and pulls us apart. He frees his head and his face is bloody with a huge blood blister between his front teeth. It's recess and the entire school is gathered as we are marched to the building and Mr. Dupuis who teaches both of us.

He looks at Couvier and then at me. "You guys can finish this in the gym if you want."

"I'm game," Couvier says.

"I've had enough," I answer. Because I'm exhausted, emotionally drained. "If he wants to fight me, he can find me."

I'm mildly concerned that he will come after me one day. But he never does. In fact, he hardly ever speaks to me from that day on.

And the strand continues to stretch as I am pulled along. The schoolyard and the kids and the fear in my belly are reaching out for something, a place to settle. And they find one.

Age seventeen and I have been playing hockey since I was five. I am playing Juvenile for Newcastle, my home town. I had told my coach at the beginning of the season that I wanted to play Intermediate. I was too big for Juvenile and all the guys were taking cheap shots at me during the games. I was constantly in fights and getting penalties.

"Your team needs you," he tells me. We are sitting in his huge Chrysler two-door from the seventies.

"I quit," I said.

"You're the best defenseman in this town. We need you." His pipe is softening the air with aroma and the dash light is friendly.

"All right," I say and exit the car. I don't know why I agreed. I don't even know why I play hockey. Before every game I lie on my bed and get the shakes. I get in a fight almost every game. But I go out and begin another season. We are playing Port Hope and I am standing in the slot to shoot at the net. The puck is loose and I go for it. I am not digging at the goalie but the goalie says I am and two guys are on me and I am on the ground and they and the goalie are going at me with fists. The ref, a big guy with a big nose and wide mouth, stoops over me and pins me as if I am the agitator. And the goalie lands three to my face. I struggle to get up and look at the ref, infuriated. "You held me down! You let them get at me!"

"To the box, mister," he says and points.

The penalty box is next to our players' bench and my coach, Mr. Flynn, hears me when I say to the ref on the ice in front of us, "I'll get you for that. That was unfair. I'll get you for that."

He laughs and half turns toward me. "You're too big for your britches, kid."

The strand of gum has grown bristles and the static electricity is arcing inside me like in a vacuum tube and I feel the anger. It's all the things I despise energizing, readying to blow a hole through my sides. And I don't know why.

The finals of that year. Four hundred people fill the arena. Newcastle and Keene are playing, very evenly matched teams. This is game seven and the series is tied. Three of the games have been decided in overtime.

I am on the ice with our first line. A fight erupts. My friend we called Phil Esposito is swinging at his opponent who is looking for an in to Phil's face. They engage and throw a few punches but the crowd is cheering and the place is loud and raucous. The refs break it up. The big ref is there but I have long forgotten the Port Hope scenario. He points at three of our players and three players from the other team. "Go," he says. "Majors for all of you." Two of them were the scrappers but why the other four? I am the captain and I skate up.

"Why are the others being penalized? Only two of them got in the fight," I ask.

"Standing too close to a fight," he answers defiantly.

"Standing too close to fight? Who's ever heard of that? Show me that in the rule book."

"Shut up or game misconduct for you," he says to me, turning away and skating toward the penalty box.

"But I am the captain. I get to question your calls."

"Game misconduct for you!" he says and turns and points in my face and I hit him in his and down he goes on his ass, holding his nose as blood gushes through his fingers and onto the ice, leaving evidence of what an asshole he is. But he's on his feet as fast as he fell and the other ref is gathering Kleenex from his pockets and passing it to his colleague as he attempts to stop the blood.

And I turn and look at all the faces of friends and friend's families who are on their feet shouting and applauding. And as my eyes meet theirs, they look back at me with horror. One by one they quiet and sit down. Time has stopped. Momentum has taken me and the unthinkable has occurred. It reverberates throughout my life. I have hit a man and hurt him. I turn to leave the ice. The second ref intercepts me, skating into my path but keeping a safe distance.

"That was a cheap shot."

"Well then, let's you and I make it fair, toe to toe, right here and now."

And he skates away. I exit the ice and head for the dressing room. Coach Flynn meets me there.

"I never thought you'd do it!" he says.

"Neither did I." I shake my head and sit down.

"No, that ref! You told him you'd get him back."

And the memory slides back into my mind of Port Hope and his big ugly face over me while the other team takes cheap shots.

"I didn't remember," I say to Mr. Flynn. He is shaking his head and snickering. His green Newcastle jacket and his balding head, the rubber mat on the floor and the benches bolted to the concrete brick walls, the smell of stale sweat and hockey bags strewn about, these images I gather because this will be the last time I will be among them.

A police officer comes and by then I am out of my gear and in my clothes, ready to go.

"Why would you hit a ref?" he asks.

"I just lost it," I answer.

"I spoke to Joe Garney, and he said this is not normal behaviour for you. He says you're a good kid. Are you willing to apologize to the ref?" Joe's our coach and also a Durham Regional cop.

"Sure. It was wrong to hit him and I am sorry for that. He is an asshole but that's not a reason to get dropped."

The period had ended and they were cleaning the ice so the refs were in their dressing room. We went to the door and the cop knocked. No one answered and he knocked again. The cop was a big guy like the ref and me, in his big Durham Regional uniform with the gold crests, holster and gun, radio and round-toed black cop boots.

"The boy wants to apologize," he called through the door.

The second ref, a smaller guy with soft hair and a moustache, cracked the door and pushed his face through.

"He will not accept an apology," skinny ref said, and the cop turned to me and asked me to return to the dressing room and wait for him, which I did. Mr. Flynn had gone back to the game and the guys were all leaving after having had the break.

Phil, who had been the fighter, came up and put his glove on my shoulder. "Fuck, Moose," and that kind of said it all. I was in big shit.

As they exited past me everyone either put a glove on a shoulder or gave me a punch in the gut, terms of endearment for the captive.

The cop returned and I was alone. "He is pressing charges. I have to read your rights. He is charging you with assault causing bodily harm, which is very serious. I should be arresting you and taking you in for a night in a cell but Joe is vouching for you, so just go home and have a quiet night, understand?"

Understand I did. I walked the dark streets with tall maples, with the wind whipping my thoughts. My old man would freak. Or would he? He had lost interest in me a long time ago. I walked in the door and he and Mom were sitting at the table.

"I hit a ref," I said.

"We know," Dad answered. "Alfie came and told us. Said the ref had it coming. He told us not to be mad, that you would be upset enough."

"Well, I got charged as well, assault with bodily harm."

That news got to him. He looked down at the table and knocked the ash off his cigarette and looked at Mom for a comment.

"She looked at me and said, "Things will work out, son."

So now I'm back, my writer self at age fifty, sitting at a desk in a house. You would think that a memory like this stands out because it is so remarkable. But it's not so remarkable. I would just as soon forget it. But the strand of gum continues to pull me. I know if I don't give in I will be tormented for days, maybe months. It has happened before. It's the danger of this game. Once you're in, you can't back out.

The next thing I know it's ten years later and I am in a Bible college class with a psychologist lady who teaches conflict management and stuff like how we keep anger slush funds in our lives. And she calls for a volunteer and I raise my hand. I'm an automaton. I have no choice. It's as if I am being controlled from another place. I am clean-cut now. I am wearing slacks and not jeans. My hair is short and I have no beard. I weigh in at 180 instead of my normal 240. I recall that I go to church on Sundays and read the Bible and Christian literature like C.S. Lewis and George MacDonald.

I go in the centre of the room, a library with a large open area. I am becoming more of myself. Everyone is sitting around on the floor. Some adults, more college-age kids, about fifteen of us. I tell a story, an emotional one, of punching a referee in a hockey game.

"We are going to dramatize this event," the prof says. Jane Anne is a redhead about my age, green eyes and not a typical Bible college professor. We have become quasi-friends, like we could date if I wasn't married and a born-again Christian. "We need some volunteers," she says. "Who will be the referee?"

My friend Sett raises his hand. He's a big guy from India. He and I have become friends during the class. When I say big, I mean he has about thirty pounds on me, which is good. The ref was that big.

"We need all the players," the prof says. She gets a few girls to be the guys on the ice in the fight. She gets a guy to be my coach. She gets another woman my age to be the second ref. She starts the play. "Re-enactment," she calls and we begin to act it out.

Everyone starts yelling and the girls, as the fighting players, start throwing mock punches while the other girls are standing close and yelling at them to fight harder. They whip it up and the emotions are a frenzy of sound. The prof gives Sett a pillow and tells him to hold it solid in front of him so I can punch it. He takes three pillows and stacks them against his chest.

"Now speak to the ref while this is all going on," the prof says.

"Tell the girls they must leave the ice, all of them," I instruct him.

"All of you, in the penalty box," big Sett says.

They look at him with wrathful faces. They are good actors and they reluctantly leave the centre of the circle.

"Why are you giving everyone major penalties?" I ask Sett.

"Standing too close," he answers.

"Standing too close? There is no such rule. Show me it in the rule book."

"Shut up," he says. He turns away and starts walking.

"You can't do that," I say to his back. "That's our best lineup. You have lost the game for us."

"Shut up or a game misconduct for you," Sett says.

"I am the captain. I get to question your calls."

Sett turns and holds the pillows to his chest and says, "Game misconduct."

"Don't forget to punch the pillow," the prof says.

And I punch the pillow hard.

"Punch it again and again and again," the prof says, excitement building in her voice. She is standing close beside me with her mouth at my shoulder.

"Again, and again," she says as I punch that pillow over and over.

"What are you saying in your head as you punch? Don't stop punching."

"Shut up, shut up, shut the fuck up!" I begin to scream.

"Who, who?" she says. "Who are you telling to shut up?"

"My father," I answer in exhaustion. My neck loses its rigidity and my chin falls to my chest. The sweet Christian lady who was acting as the second ref has been standing to the side throughout, silent, but now she comes and hugs me from the back, around my chest, and I can feel her cheek on my spine.

We all sit down and the prof asks us to express how this vignette made us feel. A few of the girls start crying. The guys look stunned and most talk about the need to forgive someone.

"The moral of the story is that you cannot really forgive someone until you know how you feel. And feelings get buried, rationalized, or pretended out of our conscious day to day lives. But they are still there, gnawing away, waiting for the opportunity for expression."

I speak out. "Scary stuff."

"Yes," she says, looking at me, and I look back into her eyes and I am back here with you typing away. And now I am being pulled again. I don't know if I can resist the urge to follow. I think it's my dad calling me somewhere. I want to follow, and if I go and experience this, I must ask myself if there was ever any option not to go. Because I went. Because I am here.

I am my old-man dying self. I am recollecting my father and the fondness I have for him, in spite of all our arguments and clashes. He died young at sixty-five. I thought we would have more time. I wonder if we will ever meet again. The old song . . . will I see you in heaven? In the cold night with the sounds of the forest, feelings are far more profound. When you are alone and people are far away and you have no phone or device to distract, you become more alive, more sensitive. Many people fear this. I learned to endure it and then to enjoy it.

I light a fire, starting with some cedar fronds and then small twigs and then gathered branches, making warmth and light. The smell of the burning is acrid and stinging and it wafts into the dark around me. I put together a small grate and a pot. I have some filtered water and I make some tea, black with sugar, all alone. Everyone's gone, died. I have outlived everyone. I remember talking to an old man when I was working in residential sales. His name was Carson and he was the age I am now, into his nineties, and he had outlived his wife, his siblings and her siblings and even his own kids. I remember him telling me how lonely it was. I am like him now. It is very lonely.

But I am remembering my father. Standing on a shore of marsh, Lake Dalrymple in the fall. Dad lighting a smoke. The canoe is nearby, the guns are in its gut, resting. The sky is pink and blue with shredding clouds and filtered sun. A wet snow is falling, pelting the leaves and the ground. The water stretches away, wide and grey.

"It's beyond describing," I say and sit on a fallen tree.

"You always were a poet, Butch." As a boy he called me Butch and would wrestle with me until I became big enough to be dangerous. I recall our lives together in an instant, like they say at death your life flashes before you.

He turns and laughs and I look up to him. His eyes sparkle like his cataracts have been removed and his dentures give a hint of the body's own humour. But I know, from my future fireside perspective, we will never be here again. We have been on so many lakes together. But we will never be father and son alone again. And by his good humour I think he knows. I think he has some knowledge he can't share because I'm not ready. But his anticipation of the day I will be makes him laugh.

The tea burns my lips. I am dying and nothing matters now but these memories, sweet and vivid. I am reliving and I am reliving and I am present and I look through my old eyes and I am present from all of time into the now. And I see my father once again, eternally once again. And as the moment fades, I realize I have recreated this scene countless times. And each time I forget that I had created it not long ago. "Longing is powerful," I say out loud to no one but myself.

So, as you can see, I am changing. And what is forward is changing what is backward. I am always more than I was. And I am changing into more of myself every day. But it is not a controlled change. In fact, it is out of control. Not that it's a bad thing, but the change is always a surprise. Should it be? I don't make things worse. I have no desire to fuck things up for myself or anyone. I guess that is the question. What am I creating? The story with all the characters was already in place when I got here, and now I influence it more than control or manipulate it. And I love my role and my cast of characters. That was not always the case. I have known hatred. Going into the future and the past has allowed me to escape from myself. Especially my relentlessly self-tortured, I-need-to-be-perfect, I-need-to-save-the-world self.

And when you escape from yourself you do become one with God, or the divine, or the essence. Maybe that is why all the bad stuff happens, so you can be released. Because the release is so exquisite. Like taking a shit after holding it for so long that you thought you would foul your pants, but instead you reach the toilet and let go, the bowels evacuating in perfect splendour. And the rush is amazing. And I guess—but this is mere speculation—that the spirit does it all for fun, for that rush, that ecstatic moment. And if I could only get that . . . and maybe I will. Maybe we all do, get that and find our release, our ecstatic moment.

And I think about the spirit, about visions and voices and I leave the campfire and the tea, just waft off on a whim, like in a dream and I am seventeen. It's so abrupt I ask myself if I am dead already. But here I am. Young and muscled with long hair. My body is like electrified jelly compared to the old bones I just left. I am at home. The old house is smaller than I remembered. My room is on the main floor with black and white naked-lady wallpaper. My mom and my aunt's idea of a cool room. And it was cool. And I remember constantly imagining having a girl like the ones on my wall with real breasts, nipples and pubic hair. There's my stereo and the gun closet with a .22 and a 12 gauge I never used. I sit on the bed before I faint.

I had moved out for a year and lived in a pink mobile home in the middle of an apple orchard but now I am back at home with my parents and a brother and sister. I drink a lot, Smirnoff and Pepsi, and I smoke a lot of dope. My buds and I do chemicals every weekend, mostly acid, some mesc, a little angel dust and if we are lucky some coke. We do a lot of bennies but those are not worth discussing. This weekend I did some dust with some chick at a party who figured out pretty quickly that I was a goof. That was Friday. On Saturday Dave had some mushrooms. And there was a party at McPhee's house. He rented an old farmhouse just outside town. You know, as I write this, I am getting high just by dredging up the memories.

We drive up in Dave's Parisienne. There are a bunch of kids partying. Lazy assholes still in school who need to get a part-time job, or just fucking drop out altogether. Dave and I have two twenty-fours of Export, but when we see the desperate multitude we hide one case under McPhee's empties in his porch and bring one case inside to distribute among the four thousand. We each take a beer and head outside and Dave takes out an oily mush-filled baggy.

"Want to do these?" he asks.

"It's like eating dog shit," I respond.

"Wash it down," he says, hoisting his stubby brown bottle.

We scoop out the mushrooms and stuff them in our mouths and wash them down quick.

"Tastes like . . .?" I ask.

"Dog shit." Dave laughs.

We leave McPhee's party, planning to return because Sugar Ray Leonard is fighting Roberto Durán and Dave's dad is hosting an old-guy's party to watch it on TV. We get there and the basement is packed with dad-friends and we are getting off on the mushrooms. The old guys are so happy to see us and they just keep handing us cold beers and laughing. The rush is amazing, old-guy friendship, sharing beers and the best fight in history. We watch Durán and Sugar Ray, toe to toe, real men battling, no fancy stuff. Tears are coming to my eyes. Sugar Ray gets a technical knockout but everyone loves Durán. Everyone loves both fighters.

"Jesus Christ," Dave says. "What a fight. Are you high, Moose?"

"Holy fuck," I answer.

We say our goodbyes. Mr. Dost is there. His son was our friend who died in a car accident. His grief has never left me. I watch him with my heightened mushroom awareness. He is severely drunk. That's what grief does, I think to myself.

We drive back to the party and I remember the beer we'd hidden. It is a revelation and I jump and holler and Dave is laughing because he had forgotten all about it. I emerge with the cardboard box to cheers and clapping. I open it on the floor and invite everyone to take one.

McPhee is staggering around, falling off of people, banging off the walls.

"Moose, Moose," he says, grabbing my shoulder. "Come here." And he guides me upstairs into an empty room. Dave follows and we stand with him in the room. "Take this," he says. "Take it." He is leaning into my face, and he is all distorted because I am so wrecked on mushrooms.

"What is it?" I say as I take a small vial. McPhee is weaving before me.

"It's a vial of acid. These kids can't find it. It will be fucking"—he waves his arm around the room—"fucking hell."

"Okay," I say, "and if we do any, I will make good."

"I trust you, Moose," he says, folding my hand around the vial. And he leaves to go downstairs to the party.

I look at Dave and he looks at me. "Wanna do some?" he asks.

"Sure," I answer. "How many?"

"Three each?"

So we each take three of the small blue pills, smaller than peppercorns, and go down to the party. But the kids are so annoying we leave.

"Where to?" I ask.

"North," Dave answers. "Let's drive north."

The Pontiac is over twenty feet long with a 350 V8 engine and four doors, chrome bumpers and bench seats front and back. It's dark and it must be November because it starts to snow as we get farther north. We are heading up east of Peterborough on Highway 7 and then north up 62 toward Bancroft.

"Where are we going?" I ask.

"Wanna go to the mines my grandfather worked in?"

"You can go in?" I ask.

"Oh yeah," Dave says. "I've been there before."

"Sounds like a trip," I answer, already tripping.

It takes an hour that seems like ten minutes until we pull into an unused road. The headlights illuminate a scrapyard-like scene, large cracked concrete pads with clumps of cedars and weeds growing through. We exit the car and I look up at the stars that swath the sky with bright white light. We walk around and inspect old machinery, large iron cocks and conveyers and even an old tractor that Dave gets on like a five-year-old kid. I walk on to the mine openings which are barricaded with boulders and old machinery.

"My grandfather was our age when he worked here," Dave says, walking up.

"They probably used horses then," I answer.

"But it only closed around ten years ago. It was going until then."

"It's so quiet, man. Did you look at the sky?"

"I love it up here," Dave says. "It's like the only place I feel I belong."

"I know what you mean," I answer. "But one day I want to feel like I belong everywhere. Know what I mean?" I turn to look at him and he is doing a wide-face smile that comes upon him when he gets really high. He has curly blond hair and a wide head. He is short and stocky and he walks that way.

"No, I don't," he answers and we both start laughing a little too hard. I can feel my head open up like the air from my lungs is escaping through my scalp.

"Watch the bush," he suggests. "The purple in between the cedars moves and becomes hallucinations."

I look and see the purple shadows begin to form shapes like people and then the shapes fill with California licence plates.

"What do you see?" Dave asks.

"California licence plates."

"California licence plates? Where did that come from?"

"Who knows, man. Maybe it's a sign. Maybe I will go to California one day. I always thought you hallucinated things that you knew. Like your brain picked up something that was already in there."

"You're weird, Moose."

"Are you seeing fazes?" I ask him. But he doesn't respond, and I am being filled by the sound of the wind in trees and the rattling of a loose piece of tin somewhere.

I am hearing sounds in the bush, animals moving. I smell creosote and diesel.

"Let's get outta here," Dave says. I nod and start walking to the car.

Back in the passenger seat, I am soothed by the green light of the dashboard. Dave asks, "What was happening back there?"

"I don't know, man. It was like we were bringing something to life."

He backs the car down the narrow path and onto the highway. There are no other cars on the road. I cannot remember the last time we saw a car this evening. It begins to snow. The flakes are thick white blotches in the headlights, forming whips of light.

"I don't know how you can drive, man," I comment.

It starts to snow hard. Soon the roads are covered and we come to a four-way stop. Dave guns the engine and cranks the wheel and we do a wide doughnut, fishtailing until the car is out of control, and Dave takes his foot off the gas to stop. I am laughing so hard my gut hurts. So is Dave. We drive on. The snow is so thick at times we are forced to a crawl. We come to another crossroads and Dave hammers the gas and cranks the wheel and around we go until again we are out of control and Dave takes his foot off the gas to stop.

We drive on farther and the snow has stopped but the roads are still slick as if they are coated with grease. Dave cranks the wheel and hammers the gas and we go around and around, but this time the car catches and the momentum sends us into the guardrail, which is actually a guard post with wire cables that attach it to other posts.

I watch that post go sailing over a steep drop, still tethered by the cables. It swings like a Scottish guy is on the other end doing a hammer throw. We stop and I look down into a ravine, a gorge over which my side of the car is suspended. Dave puts the car in reverse and guns the engine, but the tires only spit gravel. I open the door and look down. The snow-covered ground is under me but the tire is in the air. I step out carefully. Dave gets out on his side.

"Fuck," he says. "We need a tow truck."

I walk around to the front and down the bank, below the car. "I think we can get it out."

"There's no way, Moose. Even you aren't that strong."

"No, look, man," I say, "the back tires are on gravel. All I need to do is lift that front corner and the back tires will get traction and the car will pull itself out. I can rock it and then you can apply the gas when you feel traction." The chrome bumper is eye level to me. On the driver's side it has been pulled straight out from where it once curved around the front. The fender has been pushed in, almost touching the tire.

The car starts and I hear Dave: "Tell me when you're ready." I walk around and look up. His face his hanging over the open window. "I'm going to push from here," I say. "The car is too high up on the other side." I go down and put my shoulder against the bumper.

I start to rock the car back and forth with barely perceptible movement. Dave adds the gas when the car is going backwards and releases on the forward. As the movement increases I add more muscle, lifting off my legs and back, pushing and pushing and pushing until the car is rocking and then I lift and push, visualizing the opposite back tire taking weight, until the traction takes and the car accelerates backwards onto the road.

Dave puts the car in park and gets out as I walk up onto the pavement. "I don't believe it," he says. "I never thought you could get us out."

I look up. The sky is just beginning to brighten with the onset of morning. "It wasn't that hard. In fact, it was easy." I laugh. "You never know, brother, you never know what you can do."

Dave nods and we both get in the car. We drive in silence until Dave attempts a right turn and the tire rubs the punished fender. Dave stops the car. "I'll blow a tire doing that."

"Turn left and do a three-sixty until you come back to the road," I suggest, which he does and we continue on our way. There are other cars on the road now. People going to work because it is now Monday morning. I had forgotten how the bumper protrudes from the side of the car like a device of attack on other vehicles. But the people approaching us see it and veer wildly out of our way. Dave is just over five feet tall and he has taken his shoes off to drive and his left foot in a working-man sock is on the dash up by the window. As we approach vehicles in the oncoming lane we watch the faces change. The car must be in worse shape than we realize because people look horrified, open-mouthed and wide-eyed. It's too funny and we are hysterical as we drive, especially when we do the huge circle at every right turn so we can go in the right direction. We make an effort to put on a straight face during those turns, like two Monty

Python characters doing something insane which to them is completely normal.

We drive home like that and pull up in front of my house in the early morning. I go and get a sledgehammer and take three good whacks to bend the fender back in place. The mallet reverberates into my bones, but the metal does not budge. "Fuck it," Dave says, and, "See ya later."

No one is home. I go in and up to my room. My shoulders ache from sledgehammering. My body hurts from pushing the car. I lie on my bed and sink into the mattress and depression. The trip was fun, but I am empty. It's always like this when I'm alone. The highest highs and the lowest lows, this is my life. At times like this, when I am alone, I really want to end it. I know it's extreme but I really want to end this. I know if I keep on living like this I will die young.

I think of my mom and God and when I was a kid going to Mass and asking the big questions. I still talk to God. My cousins are religious. My closest cousin Kevin goes to retreats. He tells me about them. He says people have religious experiences. So, I think, I am going to ask God for an experience. And I say the prayer, "God, if there is more to this, show me now or I am just going to waste myself until I die."

I wake abruptly. The room is covered in webs. It takes a moment to accept that the webs are made of strings of light. Light webs are hanging from the ceiling and off the chest of drawers. I can't move but my heart is beating ten thousand beats a minute. And I hear a voice in my head say, "Remember what you asked?"

But I don't remember and I wait. The scene fades to normal. A voice says, "You asked for an experience. You asked if there is more. There is."

The voice has a British accent.

I AM BACK IN THE PRESENT. I wake up in this life, the real one. I am in my bed in Sunderland. "Remember, you have to pick up Danicko," my wife yells from downstairs. I almost forgot that I have this grandson, a little black kid, the result of my daughter's relationship with a man from Barbados. We started taking him on weekends when he was three to help out my daughter after the relationship with the kid's father ended. Then my daughter announced she was giving the child to children's aid for a little while. And I said, "Over my dead body." So we took him in for six months and we went to family court and hired a lawyer and the whole drama played out. It's okay now. He is with his mom and his dad sees him regularly, so it's fine.

But I don't want to tell that story now. It will bring taut emotions and overwhelm my world. I will need the support of some future story to support me, one that celebrates comedy and sees how chaos resolves into distinction.

But my grandson I love intensely, and he is in trouble frequently. He has a heart to do well. He will say, "I am going to school today and I will not get any dots." He is five and in kindergarten. And then he goes to school and does his little best and gets the dots anyway which are marks for bad behaviour.

But he has me, and I have my story of how coming close to the edge gave me the gift of who I am. And so it is with every one of us. So it is with everyone I respect and admire. None of them are the status-quo people they think they are. There is no such thing as a status-quo person. We are just individuals with incredibly diverse thoughts and lives who lend bits of ourselves to the machine called the status quo. We lend our bits to keep the machine running, the machine that is the world economy, the cities and towns, the roads and the sewers and the hydro and the internet. But go into any portion of the machine and you meet people, lovely, lively, dynamic, amazing beings full of life and drama. And this is what I mean when I say it is the light that teaches. And we all walk to the light, each of us on our own strange path. Each path as unique as a snowflake, as abundant as a blizzard. You and I are carried by the wind. I believe this. And I don't just survive by believing it. I thrive.

So last night I picked up the kid and drove him to his dad's. Today my wife is going to a horse show with a friend. I am standing in a small spring that flows under a wooden bridge near the marsh. Only my feet are in the spring. My boots and socks are on the bridge. It is six a.m. in October and the sun is just coming up. I rode my bike here. It is a short pedal from the house. The air is cold and my feet are numb because the spring is like ice.

I am wading toward the marsh. I step on a smooth round rock and crouch down. I close my eyes and the chirp of a chickadee and the rippling water catch my attention. I open my eyes and watch the colours of the leaves in decline, the muted oranges and yellows. The water is grey and slow in the channels between long grasses. I see geese. The smell of mint and soil, of decay, moss and mushrooms fills my senses. It all begins to swirl around me. Colours move in patterns like a bowl being spun on a potter's wheel. I see my life as portals on the wall of a cylinder. I see a spot. A favourite spot and I reach into it.

It is Sam Gomes's idea. My Indian friend whose birthday was on the same day as mine. He looks like an Indian on a barbershop store front with the felt hat and all, tall and straight-backed with a big nose. "Let's go see the Stones."

The only Rolling Stones record I had was the greatest hits. We played it a lot in the house four of us rented beside the Newcastle golf course. I answered Gomes, "Yeah, let's do it. Where are they playing?"

"Buffalo. Rich Stadium. Orchard Park, New York," Sam says.

We decide we need four guys to go. Sam would ask Zietz, a guy from Newtonville who hung out at the house a lot. I would ask Mike Danilko, a guy I had played hockey and worked in an apple orchard with. Mike and I had seen a few concerts together, the most memorable being Frank Zappa at Maple Leaf Gardens. And I had a car, my dad's 1970 Cutlass Supreme coupe with the 350 Rocket engine. But we didn't have any dope. Newcastle was dry. Gomes said Mrs. Lines had acid and we could pick it up on the way.

I pick up Gomes first at his house in Brownsville. It's a farm, and when I drive up he comes to the car with a backpack. When I open the trunk to put it in he sees the cooler I had bought and filled with ice for a future case of beer.

"Hang on," he says. He runs back into the porch and re-emerges with a whole chicken in his grip. It's cleaned but not wrapped, just a bare chicken carcass.

"It's fresh, man. It's not even frozen yet. You got ice."

I remove the Styrofoam lid and he throws the bird onto the bed of ice cubes. "We can roast it over the fire at the campsite."

That was our plan, to get a campsite and stay over and get to the concert really early so we could get right at the front. We pick up Zietz, with his long curly hair, tight-ass jeans, Jagger lips, tent and duffel bag. We pick up Mike last. Mike is the only one of us who has a girlfriend, and she is a very desirable girl as well. Mike did a lot of drugs before, but he has settled a bit. He would go a bit nuts on chemicals and kick in windows and shit like that. He never did it when he was with me, but people told me. He is a medium-sized guy with medium-length black hair and good teeth. He comes from a good middle-class family, like me. Both our dads work in General Motors in Oshawa.

I sit in the car after I close the trunk. Gomes and Zietz are in the back and Mike gets in the passenger side and sits in the front with me. I open the wallet key holder my dad has given me and the ignition key is missing. "Uh-oh," I say and get out and walk around the car looking on the ground. I find it in the dirt near the trunk and restore it to the key holder on a different clip.

Mike observes and comments, "Hope that doesn't happen again in Buffalo."

"Don't worry, man. It's from my old man. It's my good luck charm."

Mrs. Lines lives on the main street in town. She has two boys and a girl. The two boys are like us, only worse, and Mrs. Lines is our parents' age. I hear she does dope, but I never go there. Sam hangs out there sometimes and he tells the stories. Sam goes in and comes out and says, "She sold it all, man, but she gave me this," and he holds up a baggie with smudges and a corner filled with green acid. It looks like green candy all broken up. Like green Smarties coverings all mashed. "It's the crumbs. Acid crumbs. LSD crumbs." And everyone laughs as Mike gets out to let Sam get in, and then Mike is back in and we are on our way to Rich Stadium. We have one hash spliff which we light and pass around as we drive.

"This is going to be an amazing trip," Gomes says.

I laugh as I plug in the tape. We have one music cassette, the Beatles collection from some year to some year. Help comes on and everyone starts singing along with Lennon. And I'm thinking, it's a good theme. We may need some help before this trip is over. We'd be listening to that a lot in the next forty-eight hours.

We get to the border and wait in the long line of cars. We watch as green go-lights come on and vehicles leave the single line and drive to one of ten booths with guards who stoop out and lean to talk. We are all smirking when we drive up to our booth and our guard. She is a black lady with a cop hat and grey cop uniform and a badge and gun.

"Where are you boys goin'?" she asks in a tough voice, not smiling.

"Rich Stadium," I answer.

She lowers her head to look in the car.

"Where you all from?"

"Newcastle, Newtonville, Brownsville, Newcastle," we all answer in succession.

"Where's that?" she asks, but this time she's smiling.

"East of Toronto, east of Oshawa," I answer, looking up at her.

"Citizenship?"

"Canadian, Canadian, Canadian, Canadian," we all answer in orderly rhythm.

"Ever been to the United States before?"

"No," I answer and the others shake their heads to answer the same.

"Enjoy the concert," she says and stands up and waves us on.

"How do we get to Rich Stadium?" I ask her quickly.

Again, she smiles. "Follow the signs just here"—she leans and points—"and then once you are on the interstate follow the signs to Rich Stadium. It's pretty easy. I don't think you'll get lost."

"Thank you," I say and put the car in drive and move slowly up the ramp, past the low, flat building where cars are being searched.

"I was sure we would get searched," Gomes says from the back.

"I was hoping," Zietz chimes.

"Why? Why the fuck? We are in another country now, Zietz," I say with annoyance. "Don't get us in shit."

"We *are* in a different country, Moose. We are in Rolling Stones country."

We all laugh at Zietz's comment.

To get on the interstate we have to get off the highway and drive through the streets of the city. "This is weird. Are we sure this is the way?" But as I say this we pass a liquor store.

"Stop!" Gomes shouts, pointing.

"I see it, Gomes," I say and pull in. It is old and green like highway signs and the tiles in the ceiling are stained and the lights are like high school. We walk around like girls shopping for dresses, looking at tall bottles of booze the size of which we cannot buy in Canada.

"Look at this," Zietz says, holding up a massive bottle of vodka. The neck of the bottle is the size of a gas pump hose.

"That's a gallon and a half of American vodka," an old geezer who's been watching us says.

We all look at him as if the dead could speak. He has a greasy leather cap and greasy leather jacket on. His hair is long and greasy and his face is not pretty.

"Thanks," Zietz says with his smiling nod. "Let's get this." We all nod and head for the till, taking compressed U.S. bills out of our pockets and each laying out a ten. We reassemble in the car. No one mentions the vodka guy but I am watching the rear-view. It isn't hard to find the ramp to the interstate and we accelerate down and onto the highway.

We find the town of Orchard Park, which is beside the stadium. There are people, crowds of guys and girls like us, long-haired, jeaned, scruffy people. I drive slowly, very slowly, watching for pedestrians who are everywhere, crossing the street without regard for cars or traffic. Mike is looking for a place to park or camp or stay. But every sign says FULL or NO VACANCY with guys waving people past the motels, and as we drive out past the town where we expect the campsites to be open we see the same. Everything is full.

"Fuck," Gomes says. "Where are we going to stay?"

"Stay?" I respond. "How about where are we going to park?" And we all laugh because we are from Newcastle where we party in fields and forests, on the beach of Lake Ontario and at the end of farmers' lanes. And that is what we look for now. We drive out into the country, past farms and hayfields similar to the places where we smoke dope and party at home. Except that here there are signs that read NO TRESPASSING. TRESPASSERS WILL BE SHOT.

Undeterred, I turn into a big hayfield, one hundred acres at least, and I drive through the centre because the hay has been taken off already. At the back of the field is a clump of brush and then a hardwood forest. I pull in behind the clump of bush and park. There is a river and tall trees. I get out of the car and walk to the river's edge. The opposite side is a rising shale cliff of broken stone with cracked and crumbling ledges forming patterns of shade in the failing sunlight. The water moves slowly over the stone bottom, echoing rippling noises into the forest beyond.

Zietz wanders off into a clearing carrying the tent. He hollers, "Hey, look. There's a fire pit. Someone camps here." Gomes and Mike go to set up camp but I stay and take off my shoes and wade in. The water is shallow and warm. Even in the middle I am only up to my waist, resisting the slow push of the stream. I look far down under the canopy of tree branches. The stone is red and the water is clear and growing dark in shade. Birds call and fly across the stream in arcs like kids on a swing, down and up into the cover of the trees. The smell around me is metallic, like the taste of iron-tainted water.

"This is like a dream," I say to myself and smell wood smoke. I have wandered a good distance and realize the boys have a fire going. I wade back up the stream and stop and watch from the centre, in the dusk.

"Where the fuck is Moose?" Gomes says.

I make an owl noise.

"There he is!" Zietz says, pointing. "Moose, you crazy cunt!" And everyone laughs as I make my way out of the river to the camp.

"We've been saying we need to get some dope," Mike says. "But Zietz is drunk and says he might be sick."

"He guzzled the vodka, man," Gomes says.

Zietz is sitting on a rock and weaving like a guy in a trance.

"Okay," I say to Mike. "You and Gomes go and I'll stay here with Zietz." We all look at Zietz as he falls off the rock and onto the ground, heaving his body and puking. I throw the keys to Mike and he and Gomes get up to go, walking out of the bush to where the car is parked.

"There's no ignition key," Mike yells.

"Fuck," I say and run out while I feel around my pockets for the key.

"We found it," Gomes says when I get there. "Look."

And there it is on the floor of the car. I reach in and pick it up, take the key holder from Mike and reattach the key.

"Attach it good," Gomes says, "because I don't think you have a second key hidden somewhere."

I shake my head. "It's at home."

"Man!" Mike says and gets in the car. Gomes gets in the passenger side and gives me the thumbs-up. "Wish us luck, man."

"Okay, boys. I do. Get us some really good shit."

I watch the taillights travel and exit the field. Then I think I'd better check on Zietz, but when I get back to the fire I see he has already crawled into the tent. I think of the key wallet again. It was a talisman from my old man.

That is how I saw it. He was overprotective as hell but he always let me go on these trips. He would lecture my ass off afterward about drugs and girls and sex. "You still smoking that stuff?" he would ask with superior disdain. "Yes!" I would answer with punk attitude. Then I would hear the lecture which was usually pretty good because he would throw in stories about some of his drug-head friends at work in GM. Same with sex. "Never use a woman," he would say in a moment of over-seriousness with his thin-line angry mouth. But then he would tell us about his buddy Vexler who investigated sex with the same curiosity dad would use to approach a fishing hole.

Gomes and Mike have left, Zietz is passed out in the tent and I am sitting by the fire on a short stump in a semi-comatose state. And I dream an old man by a fire. At Park's Creek, a place I would visit as a kid with my aunts and mom. The creek is slow and covered with lily pads and weeds like a skin. The water is black and I watch through an old man's eyes the dragonflies hovering, rising and lowering in vertical lines straight as plumb, and then forward in speed like an arrow. The long body and six wings and the bulging head of eyes. The air is cold but I have a warm sweater and the boots on my feet are Grebs and on my hands are cloth gloves with the fingers cut out. And my emotions are of life lived and of loves grown over decades.

It is too much for my adolescent young adult self and I pull back, get up and walk out of the forest into the hay field, which is now soft new-grown grass. I strip naked and run. There is no moon but the stars are brilliant and a short fog is rising off the field at face level, like a mini atmosphere hovering above the ground. I run. I run fast with the dew on my skin, soaking my feet and cooling my body with condensation mixing with sweat.

I run to the end of the field and then perimeter. I feel the old man. He is still in my mind, like he is remembering and relishing this moment. I run harder until I am out of breath, exhausted and enchanted. I fall in the grass, stretch out my youth and masturbate. And I can feel the old man feeling it, feeling it all. And I realize he is me, somehow, someway, in some stretch of time. I know I am giving him something. It is vigour and youth and strength. For some reason I feel he needs it. I know feeling this youth in his bones will change him.

And I lay under the stars and try to feel him and I do. I feel protection and knowledge like wisdom. I feel peace and a part of everything around me. I sink into the soil, let the odours of earth fill me and I can smell the river and the trees it loves, like a union of moss and leaf and rock.

I SEE THE HEADLIGHTS COME OFF THE ROAD AND BOUNCE OVER THE GRASS ONTO THE FOREST WALL AND I RUN FOR MY CLOTHES. They are at the fire when I walk up. Zietz is out of the tent and sitting on the ground cross-legged with his head hanging down, his long curly hair obscuring his face. "Zietz, how ya feeling man?" I ask him, but he just groans a reply. I look at Gomes while Mike tosses the keys to me.

"Whatdya get, boys?"

"This," Gomes says, holding up a huge bag of weed. "This is an ounce, man. Five fingers and it's good. We smoked some. You should have seen it there." He drops his face toward the baggie to roll a joint.

"What was it like?" I ask Mike.

"It was crazy," he answers laughing. "People walking around with drugs, smoking and selling. With the state troopers everywhere, just leaving everyone alone. So many people, like Woodstock or something."

"We got some other shit too," Gomes says. "The guys said it was really good. Said it was THC. The chemical that gets you high in pot but on its own."

I look at Mike. I am not too keen on taking a white powder from a stranger. But Mike reads my thoughts. "He was cool. You don't have to worry. We hung out with him and he found us the pot."

"We have to get there really early," Gomes says, standing with a joint in hand. "The lineup will start first thing in the morning. We should leave here at dawn."

"I'm good with that," I say and everyone nods as Gomes lights the joint and passes it around.

"We almost got lost," Mike says. "We couldn't remember where the field was and then we were driving and we thought we saw this old guy so we slowed down and there wasn't an old guy but there was the driveway to the field. For a while we were picturing you and Zietz walking to Rich Stadium with a bottle of vodka and a tent."

We all laugh. I realize that could have actually happened. And I think of the old man, and the song lyric to Magical Mystery Tour comes into my head. It is one of the songs on the Beatles cassette in the car and it is apropos for this moment, maybe for this weekend.

At the light of dawn Sam calls to wake us all up. I have slept in the car and am already up and washing off in the river. Zietz and Sam take down the tent while Mike rolls a joint. We pass it around, standing over the spent fire from last night. "The Rolling Stones," Gomes says. He lifts the joint and blows smoke to the sky. We pass it around, each taking tokes. We are all laughing at nothing and Gomes passes the roach on a clip which is burning like a live coal. He releases the roach into the coals of the pit and says, "Let's go."

We rush to the car and Mike asks, "Got the key, Moose?"

I produce the wallet with ignition key and we get in the car, Gomes and me in front and Mike and Zietz in back. "You know the way?" I ask Gomes.

"Uh, no." So Mike gets in the front and Gomes gets in the back. We drive out of the field, up and onto the pavement. I accelerate away with Mike piloting. We get to the stadium and are driving along the main street of Orchard Park, New York when we see a guy hold up a sign that says PARK HERE. It's his front yard and for fifteen bucks we can park on his front lawn. It's five in the morning when we pull in. The streets are packed with people laughing and shouting.

"Let's snort that stuff," Gomes says, so we each take a piece of foil folded into a rectangle. We all take a straw from a box Sam and Mike bought yesterday. We expose the greasy white powder and snort it into our nostrils. It has a chemical taste like angel dust and it makes my nose run and the taste is stuck in my throat.

The world becomes instantly bright, like it was already bright but I hadn't noticed. Everything I look at is in crystal-clear focus but the edges of my vision are blurred. I am standing outside the car but I do not remember getting out of the car. Did we snort the stuff outside? A state trooper is on the street in his wide-brim hat and grey and brown uniform and he is looking straight at me. I smile but he doesn't and I look away. I look at the others. They are looking around at the people and the street.

"Man!" Mike says with a face mapped by a smile.

Gomes is smiling and moving his head from side to side.

Zietz says, "This stuff is amazing."

Gomes starts walking and we all follow. I can see the stadium down the street, a massive wall like a science fiction scene. Everything is sloping down toward me, but I realize it is only the light that is slanting and it makes everything appear concave. We stop at the four corners of the town. There is a pizza shop and a huge lineup.

"I'm hungry," Gomes says. "Let's get a pizza."

"That's a long lineup," I say.

"I'm not standing in that lineup," Zietz says.

"Fuck that," Mike says.

"C'mon, Moose." Gomes nudges me.

"We haven't eaten since Newcastle," Zietz comments suddenly.

"Okay, I'm hungry too," I answer and move into the lineup with Sam. Soon the other guys come into the line with us.

"People are coming out with beer," Zietz says.

"Let's get some beer," Mike suggests.

So we all stand in line and then we are in the store.

"Medium double-cheese and pepperoni," I say while the others pick two six-packs of American beer. I stand to the side and wait while Mike pays. A pack of people, mostly guys, is standing to one side waiting for pizza. I go and stand with them while the others exit with the beer. The guy making the pizza calls me after a while and I get the pizza and go out and sit on the curb with the others. It is six in the morning. I know that because a girl from Newcastle drove by while we were sitting there.

"You idiots," she said later on back in our hometown. "I drove right past you. I had my head out the window yelling and you just looked at me like I didn't exist."

"We were really high," I said.

"No kidding," she laughed. "It was six o'clock in the morning and you and your friends are sitting on the curb, six feet from the traffic, eating pizza and drinking beer. I said to my friends, those guys are from my town. They couldn't believe it."

"I couldn't believe it either," I answered. "Who'da thought you could buy pizza and beer first thing in the morning?"

"No, not that," she said. "That it was you guys, in Buffalo, sitting there. You were so noticeable and you were from here. I didn't expect that."

"I get you," I said. "It was weird that we were so weird."

She just nodded. She was my friend's sister and had massive tits and long thin hair that stuck to her head like a hippy's. I wish I had seen her.

We sit on that curb for a long time, watching the endless line of cars stopping at the stop sign before moving on. We drink our twelve beers and then we look at the crowds of people marching toward the stadium.

"We should be in line by now," Gomes says and stands up.

We start walking to the stadium.

"Good dope, eh?" Gomes says at my side.

"Yeah, man, it's the best. It's really clean. My body is really high but it feels good, no shitty sweats or anything."

"It's visual too," he continues. "Everything is warped."

A guy walking in front of us turns around.

"What are you guys on?"

"T," Gomes says.

"Nice," the guy says. "Lots of good drugs here. Ever seen the Stones?"

I shake my head.

"No," says Gomes.

"It's crazy. It's a non-stop party. Where are you guys from?"

"Newcastle," I answer.

"How 'bout you?" Gomes asks.

"Hamilton," the guy answers. "Everyone here is from Ontario. The Stones couldn't come to Canada because Richards got busted with heroin. They came here instead."

The guy runs ahead to catch up with some people and turns and waves. We wave back.

We get close to the lineup. It's a mile long.

"What time is it?" Zietz whines. "These people shouldn't be here."

"Fucked if I know what time it is," Mike comments and staggers.

"And why the fuck are they playing Steely Dan? I fucking hate Steely Dan," I say to the sky and everyone close by. People turn to look and then look away.

"I think the whole world is in that fucking lineup," I continue.

"You should have got up earlier," says some smartass chick at the front of the line. Her body is bending with the music and her long hair is swaying behind. She looks beautiful even though she's not.

"When did you get here?" Gomes asks her.

"I was here yesterday, honey," she answers.

"Do you like Steely Dan?" I ask her.

"Who?" she says, still swaying.

"They must be playing it for crowd control," I say to Zietz who just stands and smiles with his Mick Jagger lips.

"Let's get in line," Gomes urges.

"I'm not standing in that line," I say. "What's the point? We'll never get in."

"Me neither," says Mike. "I'll just go in after everyone has gone in."

"But we'll get the worst seats. We'll be sitting at the very back." Gomes is pulling the hair off his forehead with a fist and grimacing.

"I'm going to look around," Zietz says and Mike and I follow him. Gomes, who is acting like an isolated warrior from an ancient race, goes off alone.

Some black ladies in short hot pants and high platform shoes come over to us. They are saying something but I cannot understand a word. I turn and suddenly Gomes is beside me laughing and nodding.

"What are they saying?" I ask him.

"I think they're prostitutes and I think they're guys."

Mike is laughing a little too hard and the prostitutes are laughing at him. Their hot pants are red, white and blue and so is their makeup and I look to see if they have bulges. They walk away from us, strutting on long thin legs.

I am bumped on the elbow and Zietz is passing a joint. I take a draw and turn to offer it to Gomes but he is gone again so I offer it to Mike. We walk over to the lineup and walk down to see the people. There are lots of straights, people with nice clothes who are laughing and dancing.

"What are people like that doing here?" I ask Mike. He just shakes his head and we turn and wander back to the front. We see Sam standing at a wire fence that surrounds a field in front of the stadium entrance. Two kids who look about twelve are each sitting up on a fence post. Local kids for sure because they look like they know their way around, long-haired little punks like our little brothers who steal our dope.

"Come here, guys," Gomes calls and gestures.

We walk over and I ask the kids, "What are you guys doing?"

"Nothing, man," the one kid answers.

"Leave us alone," the other kid says. They are both looking toward the stadium entrance across the field. I look. It's about two hundred yards on a diagonal from where we stand.

"Now," the one kid says and they both jump off the fence and start running across the field.

"C'mon!" Gomes shouts and we jump the fence and run after them. The kids are running their asses off and we kick into high gear and pass them. I look behind us and security guards have jumped the fence and are following us. We run like athletes. I begin to treat it as a race. I pass Gomes and he laughs and speeds up. We jump another fence at the opposite side of the field with the kids right behind us and we charge into the front of the line and through the entrance just as they are pulling the rope across. We are among the first group in. We come to a gate and present our tickets. They are checking bags but we have nothing but T-shirts, jeans and running shoes. We walk down the wide passage under the stands, onto the field and up to the front of the stage. We are so close Jagger can spit on us if he wants. I turn and look at the empty stadium, reaching the sky and stretching away forever.

"Good job, Gomes," I turn and say.

"Yeah man!" the others chime in.

I turn to the stage, ten feet tall with huge tarps on each side reaching high, pink cloth strapped to scaffolding a hundred feet up. Boxes the size of a train are lined up in front of the stage. Roadies are up top running around getting things ready. I turn back and look at the stadium. People mill in like ants into a mound.

I sit down cross-legged like a swami and a tiredness settles on me. I can feel my old-man self, the old man in the tent. He's in his sleeping bag now. The air is cold around him but he's warm. And he's laughing at his memories that are so vivid because I am living them now. I am with him in his tent and he is with me, sitting on an orange tarp large enough to cover a football field. I am hallucinating but it's nice.

The day is hot but I only notice occasionally. We watch people crowd in around us as the morning matures, wanting to be as close to the front as possible. First April Wine appears which surprises me. I never expected a Canadian band, especially one that had played at my high school. Then the Atlanta Rhythm Section comes on, a good band and I have their album at home. People stand up and dance. There's a couple right beside me, her in jean shorts and a halter and he in blue jeans with a red Fleetwood Mac T-shirt and I wonder if I will ever be part of a couple. I am fucked up when it comes to relationships. My last one ruined me.

I met her in the library where I was doing some homework. I was the student council president. Some guy got elected but he quit because the workload was too much so they asked me and another girl, Vicki Clarke, if we would do it together. The criteria were good marks and popularity with the students. That was me, believe it or not.

Moose

So I am in the library and she comes and sits opposite me. Fine, I thought. I didn't know her but it was the library. There were other tables to sit at so I looked up.

"Hi, I'm Laura," she said.

"Ron," I answered.

Her face was expressive, with dimpled cheeks and a high forehead. I thought she was odd but cute. Her small mouth twitched with her thoughts when she did her homework and she would often press her pencil eraser into her cheek.

"Why do they call you the Moose?" she asked suddenly.

"Because of the way I play hockey," I answered.

"Do you get in fights?"

"Yeah. Some."

She was not attractive because she was good looking. She was attractive because she was spunky and had attitude—she was sexy. Her clothes would have wear-holes in the belly, or in her jeans on a thigh. She was short and compact but slinked when she walked as if to say *I am not in a hurry for anyone.*

We fell in love. She reeled me out of myself over the next six months. She disrobed my vulnerable self, took him out of his iron anger and by the summer he was naked and wanting to be tortured by love.

"I want you to be the first," she said. On a frigid night, in my warm car with headlights illuminating high snowbanks, she had me take off my clothes but just to my underwear while she took off her shirt and bra, exposing loveliness and I couldn't do a thing. We kissed. We touched, but my old man's words stopped me.

"Never use a woman," he had said. "To use her is to dishonour her." So I never pressed. She seemed disappointed, not only at that time but also at other times. I had made a room in our bare basement, with the old octopus furnace pipes keeping us warm. And she came on strong, and I knew we could have made love then and there. Or at least got close. But my mom was upstairs so I backed down. I could not get past the ideal of dishonouring my parents' home.

I never was the first. She left me a note in my locker that left me massacred by need on the last day of school. "You're a really nice guy and deserve someone better than me."

Now I am laughing. Someone older than me is speaking in my head. And I'm listening because I'm so stoned. "We have concluded," it is saying, "that a woman wants what she wants and if a man can't give it to her she will draw him out, kill him and eat him."

But it's not really funny because I had a breakdown after that. I had been student council president. I had been an honour student. I was the captain of my hockey team. But after she broke up with me, I couldn't think. My parents were always fighting and I thought they would break up. My brother was always in trouble. He hated life.

So I started into drugs, smoking dope, staying high all the time. The first time I did acid it was like meeting God. The good guy, the student, the kid with a bright future was gone.

I was a fuckup. I called myself that. It felt good. We were all fuckups, me and my friends. My motto became "dead by thirty" and I meant it.

It felt good. We were all fuckups. Even Mikey with his sweet straight girlfriend did enough dope to launch his brain into orbit.

There are a lot of fuckups in the crowd here at the front of the stage. Rough guys in groups standing and yowling to friends. "Where are you from?" a blond guy with Johnny Winter hair and some teeth missing asks me.

"Near Oshawa," I answer. "You?"

"St. Catharines," he answers. "You high?"

"A little," I said.

Journey comes on next. I like them and listen to their albums. Steve Perry, the singer, turns his ass to the crowd and pushes it around in rhythm with the music.

"What is he? A fag?" Gomes says.

"The music is good though," I answer and ignore Gomes and Steve Perry.

There is a guy beside us with a paper bag filled with firecrackers, a weird little guy with a scrawny beard and an engineer's cap and overalls with no T-shirt.

"That could get crazy if you light those things," I say to him. He smiles and nods but doesn't look at me.

I turn to Sam and say, "We should do the acid now."

"Yeah, let's," he says and taps Zietz and Mike to come into a huddle. Sam takes the baggie out and divvies up the microdot crumbs and powder onto our palms. We each lick the contents up. Everyone watches and a girl offers us a water jug to wash the stuff down.

The crowd tightens around us. I look up into the stands and the aisles are full of people coming down and sitting on the steps. People try to get out, to get up the stairs but no one gets out of the way.

We have been standing for a while. People press around us and I say to Gomes, "No way out now until the concert is over." I look at the firecracker guy.

"If those firecrackers cause a stampede, guess who gets trampled first?"

Gomes laughs and looks. A guy comes past us with his girlfriend on his shoulders, frantically pushing around us. "It's all right. It's all right," his girlfriend is saying. "What's wrong with you? Stop, let me down."

"Stay away from the brown acid," Mike says, leaning into us.

We all laugh.

Big marching-orchestra music blares out of the speakers, surprising everyone. The crowd begins to roar in response and a big voice with an English accent says, "Ladies and gentlemen, the greatest rock and roll band in the world . . . the Rolling Stones!"

The boxes in front of the stage open and ten million pink balloons rise up before the stage, spiralling into the sky. I look up to watch. As high as I can see, the balloons spiral. The stage is totally obscured and then it clears and there he is, in a white T-shirt with a graffiti painting on the front and red plastic pants that are too short, white socks and pointed white running shoes. His hands are touching and his fingers are beating a rhythm while his hips swing side to side with the slow guitar chords that fill the sky with noise like jets. His body is all angles, all parts that fit together in awkward symmetry. Big hands and a big head, big feet and a small, lean, muscled body. And every move releases the crowd into more excitement.

I turn and look around. Ninety thousand people all on their feet, clapping in sync with Mick Jagger. A massive blur, the multiple a whole, a singular orgiastic event.

This is the Jagger universe. It starts with Honky Tonk Women. Then Ain't Too Proud to Beg and then the Some Girls song where he sings, "Black girls just want to get fucked all night, I just don't have that much jam." Then Beast of Burden, When the Whip Comes Down, Shattered, Tumbling Dice and Fuck a Star from Goats Head Soup. Mick runs around, up and down the walkways that stretch out on each side of the stage, does his maniacal dance steps, throws his hips, struts and jumps, grabs Ronnie Wood by the balls. He stares into the crowd. A few times he stares at us, at me. I stare back at him, like he is a clown, or a god, or both. I am not moving or dancing. You don't do that if you are from Newcastle. Gomes or Mike or Zietz aren't dancing or clapping either. We just stand. Gomes looks at me and laughs, leaning to my ear.

"He's insane, man!"

I nod agreement.

Richards stands with his guitar and weaves and bobs. Wood runs around with his, smoking cigarettes as he plays. Wyman plays bass with a stone face and Watts drums like a monkey in a trance. But Jagger is sticking his hands down his crotch and flapping the front of his stretch pants. A bra sails into the air. And other articles of clothing—shoes, shirts, panties—fly toward the stage. I am packed in by bodies so tight I can lift my feet off the ground and be supported. Jagger dodges plastic bottles and more shoes. He is fast. He runs to the far side and runs back.

He's so fast. A bottle flies and just misses as he ducks. His anger is apparent as he runs to the other side of the stage. He comes back again and stoops to the crowd. A guy has a bottle lifted and I grab it and throw it to the ground. The guy looks at me and shrugs, but Jagger seems to notice and waves his finger toward me, nodding in the rhythm. Our eyes lock for the briefest moment before he skips away.

"He looked at you," Gomes yells into my ear, and I nod.

"Yes, he did. I felt shivers up my back," I yell back into Sam's ear.

They roll through the songs Happy, Miss You, Brown Sugar. They play some Chuck Berry stuff, Sweet Little Sixteen. The intensity has built, the momentum is in full swing. Ninety minutes have passed. Jagger has stripped off his shirt and Jumping Jack Flash is running from the back of the stage and leaping through the air, landing and doing it over again, soaked with sweat and the crowd is a roar of ecstatic feverish joy.

And it's over.

The Stones gather at the front of the stage. "Goodnight Buffalo!" Jagger hollers into the mic with his English accent. And they leave and the stage is empty. The crowd roars in response. The call of the vanquished, I think as I stand and look around. Our god has left, left us empty of our offerings. Our fevered emotions have been sacrificed and he is fed and gone and he is not coming back. But I feel wonderful. Without my angst and my fears and failures, I stand in an eternal moment. It is the first time I will feel this way. It will be my secret place for the rest of my life. It will enable me to do anything. For in this place, nothing matters. Nothing you do or ever will do exists here. This is freedom. This is where the gods dwell eternally, bobbing in and out of reality at will. And Jagger brought me here.

Ninety thousand people stomp and yell and clap for the encore. On and on they cry for more. I have no sense of time. The noise is forever, like an ocean, like a waterfall, like a river crashing. It dims, it dies. People start leaving. The stadium is draining like a bathtub, from the top down, sinking people into the exits.

We stay, stand in the empty floor, the pink tarpaulin a garbage dump of clothing, blankets, plastic jugs and pools of liquid. There is a crowd yelling at the stage.

"It's still daylight," I hear a guy holler. "It's July 4th. It can't be over. Bring back the Stones!" But the roadies are about their business taking down the equipment.

A guy, skinny with a beard and long hair, shirtless in jeans with no shoes, rushes the stage, jumps and grips the edge, climbs up.

"That guy's amazing," Mike says. We all nod, gawking open-mouthed at the feat of gymnastics just witnessed. The guy is up on the stage and he turns to the crowd. Everyone cheers. The roadies grab him and madly toss him off. The people on the ground break his fall.

"It's over!" one of the roadies yells, leaning to the crowd. "Go home."

But three guys rush the stage and jump, grabbing the edge. Two fall off but one gets up. The roadies are on him, punching him in the sides and back, three against one and they throw him back off the stage. Guys keep trying and sometimes one of them makes it. But the roadies are now kicking the guys before they can even stand up.

We hear yelling from a far distance and look. Another guy has jumped from the stands onto a sound tower. He jumped twenty feet and is over a hundred feet off the ground. There is no way down. Security guys are on the steps. They have to pull themselves up to look over a concrete wall. The guy is hollering at them and dancing, taunting them.

"He is stuck, man. No way down," Zietz says.

I am laughing, laughing so hard I feel my brain splitting apart inside my skull.

"Let's walk around," Gomes says.

"I'm freaking out," Mike says. "I gotta get outta here. It's too gross." And it is. It stinks. I wonder how many of those 90,000 people pissed on the floor because they couldn't get to a washroom.

A girl walks past us with nothing on but a guy's overalls. I can see her ass through the sides and her nipples are barely covered. A tall guy in his boxers walks beside her. Zietz and I stop to watch her but Gomes and Mike keep walking. We follow them out the stadium exit into the parking lot and down the street, retracing our paths from this morning.

We get to the car and it has a flat tire.

"You have a flat," Gomes says.

"I forgot to put air in it. It has a slow leak," I say. "Let's change it."

They stare at me. "I'm not changing a tire," Gomes says. "Fuck that."

"Then you're fucking walking," I say and pop the trunk.

Mike rushes and takes the jack and Gomes takes the tire wrench and I take the tire and Zietz rolls a joint. The spare is an old bald snow tire.

"What's that?" Mike says, laughing and pointing.

"It should get us home," I answer.

We change the tire and I look at the cooler as I throw the old tire in beside it.

"Hey Gomes," I call out. "Your chicken is still in the cooler." I laugh and close the trunk.

Our plan was to stay the night. To party here and go home tomorrow but everyone is leaving. The party ended and the exodus has begun. It is hot and humid and Orchard Park, New York is as much a garbage dump as Rich Stadium.

"Let's go," I said.

"Do you know the way?" Zietz asks.

"Follow them," Mike says and points. Cars are filling the street and everyone has an Ontario licence plate.

"Let's go," I say and we get in the car and join the line of cars heading for Canada.

We drive at ten miles per hour, listening to the Beatles over and over. We make it onto the interstate but the traffic is still just taillights in a writhing red column that stretches as far as we can see.

"Look," Zietz says, reaching and pointing over the seat. "The guy in front of us is overheating." Gomes and Zietz laugh, but Mike and I are in the front and see the red light in the dash.

"It's not him, it's us," I say calmly.

"What?" Gomes says and pulls himself up to look. "Oh fuck," he says and collapses back.

I pull over. "Don't turn it off," Mike says too late. We have all experienced my car overheating and the subsequent dead battery. I turn the key and the starter just clicks.

"We need to fill the rad," I say. "By the time we do that the engine will have cooled enough to start."

"And how are we going to fill the rad? We don't have a jug," Mike says, shaking his head.

"We have the vodka bottle," Zietz exclaims, hoisting the half full bottle up for us all to see. There is a joint floating in it. An earlier plan was to soak a joint in vodka and retrieve it, let it dry in the sun and smoke it. But we couldn't retrieve it. We all get out of the car. I dump the booze out and head for the houses on the opposite side of an eight-foot wire mesh fence.

"Hang on. I'll come with ya, Moose," Gomes says and runs up beside me. I toss the bottle over the fence into the long grass on the opposite side and scale the wire. Gomes follows and we pick up the bottle and walk up to a house where we see a garden hose on a tap at the front. I knock on the door and a young clean-cut man answers.

"Our car is overheated. Can we get some water from your tap?" I ask.

"Sure," the guy says. "I don't think I have anything to give you to carry it in."

"That's okay. We have this," Gomes says and holds up the vodka bottle. The guy laughs.

"Take as much as you want," he says and closes the door. We fill the bottle and run down, climb the fence and walk to the car. Zietz is smoking joints and passing them to the cars in traffic. People are willingly taking tokes and passing the joints back as Zietz asks if they have booster cables. I open the hood, remove the rad cap and pour in the water and run back to rescale the fence, refill the bottle and repour the contents into the rad. Gomes is with me as we do this six times. As we approach the car with the sixth filling, Zietz is calling me.

"Moose, Moose, this guy has cables."

I see a guy who looks like us doing a three-point turn in a Chev Malibu to face my car. I pour the contents in the rad, reaffix the cap and get in the car. Mike and the guy have the cables hooked up and I open my key wallet and the ignition key is not there.

"C'mon, Moose," Mike calls, but I step out of the car and say, "The key is missing."

The three of them moan with despair while the guy boosting me looks bemused.

"Hang on," I say to him. I walk into the long grass thirty feet from the car, stoop down and pick up the key. I walk back to the car and sit in it and the guy says "go," and I insert the ignition key and the car turns over and starts.

"You found it?" Gomes says and leans into the car. "You're fucking with us. You never lost it."

"But I did," I say. "And then I walked over there and picked it up in the grass."

I look at Gomes. "I just knew where it was."

We thank the guy who gave us the boost. Zietz gives him some joints and he turns his car around in the traffic. People stop with courtesy and wave to let him in. We wave too and get in the car. I see a ramp and pull off and turn into the streets of Buffalo.

"Aren't you afraid of getting lost?" Mike says.

"If I stay in that traffic the car will overheat again," I point out.

"This is awesome, Moose," Sam says from the back.

"Do not light a joint, Zietz. Not here," I say, looking at him in the rear-view.

"Got ya, Moose," he replies.

"How will we find our way to the border?" Mike asks.

"We will ask directions," I say, looking out into the street as I slow for a stop sign.

I proceed slowly. Everyone is outside in the night. People walk with beers in hand. The houses are shabby and dark and need paint.

"This is a bad version of Oshawa," Zietz says.

The people are dark, not negro but dark like Mexicans.

"I think this is a Puerto Rican neighbourhood," Gomes says.

"How the fuck do you know that?" I say, laughing over the wheel.

"Just guessing," Gomes says with an ear-to-ear Indian smile. I turn my head to look at him. His black eyes sparkle in the oncoming headlights and he leans forward between the seats.

"Look out, Moose!" he says and I slam on the brakes. A guy is standing in the street in front of the car. A big guy, and he comes around to the driver's side. My window is down. He has a beer in his right hand and he leans on the car with his left.

"Hey Canadians," he says. "What are you doing here?"

"We're lost," Mike says from the other side.

"Do you know how to get to the border?" Zietz asks from the back.

He pauses and leans back to look around, over the car and up and down the street.

"Wait," he says and points. A series of pops like gunfire erupts in sparks and colours.

"Wow," I say. "That is the best."

The guy slaps the hood of the car and leans in. "Go down here four sets of lights and turn right. Then go four more and turn left. You will see it is a huge street, six lanes wide. That will take you to the Peace Bridge." He laughs a big-tooth laugh and says, "Happy Fourth of July, gents."

"Oh yeah, it's the Fourth of July," Gomes says. "That's why everyone is out partying."

I drive down to the four sets of stoplights and turn right. "He did say to turn right?" I ask the others.

"Oh yeah, oh yeah," Zietz says. "And then drive up here and look for the big street."

"And then turn left," Mike says.

"Yeah, yeah. That will take us to the Peace Bridge," Gomes says.

The main streets are deserted and I drive up to the lights and turn left and then along the wide empty lanes. Sure enough, a sign comes into view with the familiar green background and white reflective lettering. Except that the sign is the size of an apartment building and it says PEACE BRIDGE with a huge arrow pointing left.

And there is a guy with long hair down to his ass in an army jacket and jeans and work boots stopping every car. There is a lineup and we wait and watch. The cars speed away from him like they are annoyed. Then he comes to my driver's window.

"What's up, man?" I say with annoyance.

"I'm looking for the Peace Bridge but no one will talk to me."

He has this little Honda idling at the side of the road. I look at the car, at him and at the guys in my car. Everyone is snorting and laughing.

"You're kidding, right?"

"No," he says. "What is funny?" He seems annoyed with me now.

"Look!" I say and lean out the window and point to the sign.

"It says Peace Bridge and it has a huge fucking arrow. Don't tell me you never saw that?"

He stands stunned, looking at the sign like it's a plane crash.

"Thanks, man," he says and walks to his car. He gets in, never taking his eyes off the sign. I let him cut in front of me in his piss-pot car. He waves and accelerates up the ramp.

We drive around and up the same ramp to the border guard and his little shed. The border is deserted.

"Where did everyone go?" Gomes says from the back.

"Fucked if I know," I say as I roll down the window.

"Fucked if you know what?" the guard says. His uniform is green and he has no gun. He looks more like a guy that works for the Ministry of Natural Resources. Except they have guns.

"Oh," I say, looking up. "We were in a traffic jam and we had to turn off. We wondered where all the traffic went."

He just shakes his head and frowns at me.

"Where you been?" he asks.

"The Rolling Stones," I answer.

"How long were you in the States?"

"Since Friday."

"Did you purchase anything?"

I look in the back. The bottle of vodka is at Zietz's feet.

"A bottle of vodka but it's filled with water now."

"I won't even ask," he says.

"Anything in the trunk?"

My eyebrows lift and I turn and look at Gomes in the back seat. Mike is snickering to himself in the front.

"Oh no!" Gomes moans.

"What is in trunk?" the guard asks.

"You do not want to know what is in the trunk," I answer him.

"Yes, I do," he answers back. I reach to pop the trunk from the button inside the glove box and see the lid rise in the rear-view mirror. I get out and walk back. The guard is a young guy in his thirties. I like him and I hope he has a sense of humour.

He sees the cooler.

"Open the cooler," he says.

"You do not want me to open the cooler," I say.

"Just open the cooler," he demands.

"Stand back," I say and lift the Styrofoam lid, never expecting the stink to be so awful. I stoop and retch. The guard steps back, holding his nose.

"Put the lid on. Put the lid on!" he says which I do.

"How long has that chicken been in there?" he asks in a nasal voice.

"Since Friday," I answer. "We keep forgetting about it."

"Get out of here," he says and goes into his booth. I get in the car and drive away. I start laughing. I can't stop. Everyone laughs. A numbness like needles is all over me. I am out of my body and Mick Jagger is before me.

"You are the magic," he says and dissolves and I am back in my body leaning on the steering wheel, catching my breath. I sit back and press the gas, moving forward, looking behind to see if the guard might have summoned the cops because of our strange behaviour. But everything is calm in the rear-view.

10

"I'M HUNGRY," ZIETZ SAYS. "I know a Chinese place close by. I used to live here."

"No shit?" I answer. "I'm in for that."

"Me too," Gomes says.

"I'm in," Mike says.

"Where to, Zietz?" I ask.

"St. Catharines," he says.

The only thing we have eaten in the last thirty-six hours is a pizza. So I say to Zietz, "Where do we go?"

"Just keep driving. I'll tell ya." We are on the Queen Elizabeth Way. It dips into a slot like a racetrack between residential streets.

"Next one, Moose," Zietz says and I slow and turn off when I get to it. The street is four-laned with a leafy canopy.

"Keep an eye open, Moose. It's just up here," Zietz says, peering along the sides of the street.

"What is it? Is it in a house?" I say.

"Yeah, yeah, Moose. It's a house they made into a Chinese place."

Gomes and Mike are leaning over the seat.

"Is that it?" Mike asks, pointing.

"No, that's not it," Zietz says, leaning toward the dash.

"There it is." I press the brakes until he says, "No, that's not it. Never mind. It's just up here."

"Is that it?" Gomes says, pushing the seat from behind me.

"For fuck's sake, Gomes," I grunt.

I move slowly up the boulevard.

"I think that's it. Yup, that's it," Zietz says, pointing to my left.

"Turn here," Gomes and Mike say, pointing to my right because I have already passed the driveway. So I turn right from the centre lane and drive into a car that is travelling on the inside lane.

"Fuck," I say and pull ahead of the car and over to the side. I put the gearshift in park and leave the engine idling. I get out and walk back. So do the other three. I look at the car I just ran into. It is a blue Rambler, old and dented all over. The bumper is twisted up at a forty-five-degree angle. I think that was what I did but I can't be sure.

"That car looks like it's been in a derby," Mike says, but we all turn at him to be quiet. A small lady with black frizzy hair gets out of the car. She has a white T-shirt and runners and she's our parents' age. Gomes is becoming emotional, looking around, wiping his face. The others start to smirk and I have to look away.

"We are really very sorry," he says to the lady. "We didn't see you. Were you hurt?"

I want to say that we were only going ten miles per hour but I don't.

"This car is a gift from his dad." Gomes looks at me.

"Yes, that's true," I say, nodding.

"And his father will be very upset to see the scratch in the very special paint job." Gomes is running his hand down the fender.

"And look at your car," he says. I look at Mike and Zietz with a shrug as Gomes leads the lady by a gentle hand on the shoulder to inspect her own car. "Your car is full of dents and it's old. I'm sure you will be getting a newer one soon."

"Yes, you're right. I had planned to." She is looking into Gomes's face like she likes him.

"Please, can we just let it be that he fixes his car and you can drive yours like it is until you get the new one?"

"Okay." She is nodding. She turns to us and then back to Gomes. "Okay, boys. Just be careful. Okay?"

"Thanks lady," Mike says and jumps into the car.

"Yes, thank you," I say and Zietz smiles and waves. Gomes shakes her hand and then hops in the front seat. We wait for her to drive around us and then I do a U-turn into the parking lot of the restaurant.

We get out of the car and begin to ascend the stairs.

"That was a nice lady," Zietz says.

"You were amazing, Gomes," Mike says and I grab Gomes's neck and give it a faint massage. We enter and the place is dark. It is a converted house, an old wood house, and the living room and dining room are full of tables. Chinese guys in white jackets and caps like sailors emerge from the back smiling like we were expected. The place is empty except for them and us.

"Are you open?" I ask.

The leader nods and smiles and indicates the way with a bow. We sit down at a big round table covered in a draping white tablecloth. The Chinese guy puts a menu in front of each of us. And then another Chinese guy puts water in our glasses.

"Do we have enough money?" Mike asks. We each dig in our pockets and throw crumpled bills on the table. I count it.

"There's over three hundred U.S. Do you take U.S.?" I say to the Chinese water pourer.

He smiles and nods.

We begin ordering. We order two beers each. Each of us has something he wants and we order it. A different Chinese waiter is writing, filling the paper and flipping it over and filling it again. The Chinese water pourer returns with the original Chinese guy carrying a table which they set down beside ours.

"I think we ordered enough," Gomes says, laying down the menu.

We all nod and put down our menus as well. The Chinese order taker is nodding again.

"Yes, yes, you have enough," he says. He leaves. They have all gone into the back somewhere.

"How many Chinese guys are there?" Mike asks.

"They make them here," Zietz says and laughs. We all laugh. I get up to go to the washroom.

Chinese Guy One points down the stairs. I go down into the dank mouldy smell and find a clean toilet and sink. I take a leak and wash my hands and face several times. I can hear a ruckus upstairs. It sounds like another crowd of late nighters has come in. I pause and listen harder. There are only three voices: Gomes, Mike and Zietz. But they are talking and laughing loud enough to be ten people.

I go back up the stairs and look down the hall. A room full of Chinese guys are standing around a table. One turns and sees me. He smiles and waves and I wave in return. I go to the table and the food is arriving as I sit down.

"They have a huge poker game going on back there," I say. "That's why there are so many of them."

"Makes sense," Zietz says. "Chinese love to gamble."

Plates keep arriving, piled high with rice and bean roots. There are bowls with meat in greasy sauce and spareribs glazed with honey and breaded things. More bowls with sauces on their own are placed in the middle. The bowls fill our table and the table beside us.

"These bowls are really nice," I say. "This is a classy place."

"I told ya, Moose. This is the kinda place rich people come to," Zietz says as he fills his plate.

"It's called china," Mike says.

"Huh?" I say with a mouthful.

"China, Moose. The plates are called china. You know, pottery?" Zietz is laughing at me.

"You're pretty smart but you're really dumb sometimes."

We are all laughing. I look over at the door to the kitchen and poker room. Our hosts are laughing too. They love us. I love us. Right now, we are like superbeings. Anything could happen and we would skip around it.

Talking stops as we sit and spoon and fork our way through the food until it all disappears, leaving scattered remnants of rice and crumbs, peas and smears and puddles of sauce.

"Fuck I'm full," Zietz says.

"For sure, man," Gomes adds.

"I can hardly keep my eyes open," I say.

"I'll drive, Moose," Zietz says.

"Okay Zietz," I say and we pay and leave a couple of twenties as a tip. There is a lineup of Chinese men saying goodnight and shaking our hands. We each bow, not as a joke, on our way out. We make our way to the car and I give Zietz the keys. It's not until we are back on the QEW that I realize my mistake.

"How fast are we going?" I ask Zietz, but Mike responds instead.

"Ninety."

"Pull over, Zietz," I say. He does.

"Sorry, Moose. I didn't know I was going that fast."

"It's okay, man. We're all tired. Shove over." He moves over into the passenger side and I get in the driver's seat and pull back onto the highway. I turn off on a service road and onto the shoulder and turn off the car.

"We sleep here," I say and pop the trunk. I get out, walk around and grab a pillow. Gomes is beside me reaching for his.

"I'm sleeping in the grass," I say.

"I figured," he answers. "I'll do the same. Zietz and Mike are already stretched across the seats in the car."

I go and lie down in the grass. Gomes is a few feet away. I look at the sky full of stars. It's a warm night and the grass is soft. The highway is quiet. I stretch out my legs, release a long breath and I am gone. Exhaustion is my peace.

And I dream. I am looking at the stars but my eyes are closed. The grass is touching my cheeks but I cannot move to brush it away. I am feeling love. How I love these guys I am with. How I love the border guard and the couple that danced when the Atlanta Rhythm Section were playing. I love the Chinese guys and the lady we crashed into. I love Mrs. Lines and I love the old guy in the liquor store who scared me. And I love Mom and Dad in Newcastle and I love the American border guard with her gun and her hard-won smile.

I love life and I realize I will always love life, whatever happens. I can hear Gomes snoring. Sam Gomes who has the same birthday as me.

Things are changing. There is movement toward something, somewhere, a new place or time. I am moving. I can feel it. Something is changing. Duck brings mescaline to town. Everyone does some. Ted and Millson do some. These guys are neighbours and have been my friends since Grade 1.

I enter the dream. We all enter the dream. People start talking to people who aren't there. It's the mesc. It's the first time we ever did chemicals. We are all together on the dirt road smoking joints around a Chev Biscayne. Ted is telling us how he woke up his mother in the middle of the night by banging and shouting in his basement bedroom. How she came in saying, "Ted! What's wrong?"

"Get out," he said and took her hands and pushed her backward and out the door which he closed and locked. But the light came on. The switch was on the outside. He saw speaker wires dangling across a mirror. Those were the snakes. He saw psychedelic posters of shapes and colours. Those were the spiders. He opened the door quite calmly.

"Ted. What's wrong?"

"I smoked some bad pot, Mom."

We all laugh and Millson tells us how at dinner he was shouting at his peas to shut up.

"Shut up," he had said to his dinner plate.

"What, Dale?" his father asked while Dave his brother kicked him under the table. "Shut up, shut up," Dave whispered. "It's the mesc."

Ted then tells how on a backroad he pulled over and opened the trunk looking for us. He could hear us laughing and concluded that since we were not in the car we must be in the trunk playing a joke on him.

I tell them how I just about crashed into Philip Dost at the box factory stop sign. "Drove right through it," I said. "Saw him later and he said, fuck Moose, are you crazy, I almost crashed right into ya."

We are high for two days. On Sunday I go to work pumping gas at the Esso on the 401. Zietz works there.

"Did you hear, Moose?"

"Hear what?"

"Philip Dost died."

"What? Dusty?"

"He drove his car under his neighbour's eighteen-wheeler."

"Mr. Innis?" I say, leaning with my words.

"Yeah. Dusty was coming down the hill. He wasn't going home. He was going past. The other two guys lived, but Dost broke his neck. They must have seen it coming, but he didn't."

I go and sit down on the vinyl seats in the lobby.

"I guess the guy backs his truck up across the highway all the time. They have those long driveways up there past the hole in the wall. He had the flashers going. His wife even had a flashlight and was in the road waving it. Dost never saw it. He smashed right under."

"This is a fucking nightmare," I say and put my face in my lap.

"I guess you knew him?" Zietz says.

"Yeah. We played hockey together since we were kids. And I partied with him. And I know his parents. Mr. Dost has driven us to games. And Mr. Innis was my hockey coach and Mrs. Innis drives the school bus. I know their son Jimmy. We played hockey on the same team."

"Sorry, Moose."

"Thanks, Zietz."

I pause and then ask, "Do you think he killed himself?" I ask the question because I am thinking of death and how many times I have contemplated suicide. I think it is normal to want to kill yourself and that it's just natural instinct that prevents us.

"Those last few seconds would have been hell. I don't think so, Moose. I think he froze. I think he freaked and couldn't move."

I nod and see a car pull up to the pumps. "I have to get that."

"See ya later, Moose."

"For sure," I say and push open the aluminum-framed lobby door with my shoulder. I walk up to the car as a lady rolls down the driver's window.

"Fill it up with super, please," she says.

I don't answer and look at her. I don't understand her.

"Pardon?" I say.

"Fill it up. Super." She turns toward the steering wheel and then cranes her neck out to look back at me. "Are you on drugs?"

"No. My friend died in a car accident. I just found out."

"Oh my god," she says, and, "Oh my god."

She doesn't look back again. The car is a new Cadillac, very long and shiny with chrome bumpers, rims and a soft roof. I fill the tank and walk up. "Twenty-three," I say.

She passes me forty and turns. "Keep the change, honey." She grabs my fingers with hers as the bills pass to me. I look at her and her cheeks are wet. Then she turns and drives out the lane and down the ramp. I go in the kiosk and just throw the forty bucks in the till. I can't even count out the tip.

I go in and sit down in the office. The glass front affords a view of a wide parking lot with eighteen-wheelers idling and truckers either sleeping in the cabs or eating in the restaurant. The parking lot lights are tall cranes with glowing heads and the highway is empty. It's two in the morning when another car comes in. I walk out like a zombie and nod to the driver and fill the tank, stand in the booth and take the cash, give the change and walk back up the steps and into the office, still like a zombie. I think about Dusty.

The last time we partied was at Oscar's. He has a room separate from his house with its own entrance, in an attic that looks like an old bell tower. We smoked dope and played the music loud. Oscar turned off the lights and put on a strobe light and we danced and played air instruments. I had to leave to come here to work, because I work steady midnights.

I pull the vinyl and chrome seats out onto the patio. The night is warm and I nap off and on. Tanya who is a cook in the restaurant comes out for a smoke break and sits beside me. She lives in Brownsville and knew Dusty. She lights a cigarette and leans on my shoulder, not saying a word, but I understand and let her.

The next day I see Oscar uptown and he asks me if I am going to the funeral. I say I am and that Ted and I are going and we can pick him up if he wants.

"Dusty and I just about ran into you on Saturday, Moose. You pulled out right in front of us," Oscar says.

"Yeah. I did some of the mescaline that was going around. I saw Dusty in town later on and he gave me a rough time. Who would have known that was the last time I would talk to him?"

Oscar just turns his head quickly like he is taking a whiff of air and walks away.

On the day of the funeral I am sitting at our kitchen table looking out over the small meadow that is our side yard. A cardinal is perched in one of the old apple trees. The stark red is a contrast to the grey and green.

"You can't go to a funeral dressed like that, son," my mother says.

Our big cop friend Gibby is sitting at the table with me. He is in his OPP uniform. He often stops in for coffee when he is working. I have already been to his farm with him to pick up his Chev Impala. He is lending it to me for the funeral because it has air conditioning and a nice interior.

Moose

"Death is hard to see," he has warned me.

I am wearing a nice T-shirt and jeans with Hush Puppies soft-soled shoes. I thought I looked pretty nice. I look at Mom.

"What do I wear?"

"Borrow one of Dad's shirts and ties from work. And borrow a pair of his slacks."

I look at our cop friend and he slowly nods.

"No way," I say. "No tie."

"Ted will be wearing a tie," she says.

I go in the living room and sit at the phone chair and call Ted. Ted's dad and my dad work together in GM. Ted's dad was the reason my dad moved our family to Newcastle. I was only four. Ted was my first friend except for my cousins.

"Ted. You wearing a tie?'

"We have to, Moose. Out of respect for the family."

I hang up and go into my parents' closet and take out blue slacks, a blue short-sleeve dress shirt and a blue clip-on tie. I walk out to smiles of approval, get the cop's keys and head out the door. I drive up the street to Ted's and pull up and honk. Ted comes out in the same attire as mine, only brown. He gets in the front seat.

"Fuck," I say and he laughs. We drive uptown to Oscar's, pull up on the street and honk. Oscar comes out in a grey suit with a red tie, cufflinks and a new haircut. Oscar is dark like an Indian even though his parents are white. And Oscar is beautiful. I think most guys are ugly but not Oscar. His hair is black and shines like the hide of a well-groomed horse. His teeth are white and straight and his face is clean and proportioned like a fine-looking woman's, with long black lashes and high cheekbones and a neat nose that fits his face. Only his chin is square and manly like his body which is square and large like a running back. He gets in the car and I start on him.

"Fuck, Oscar," I say, looking in the rear-view. "You make us look bad."

"You two look like a couple of geeks applying for a job at GM," he says. He has a voice like Lou Reed and I like to hear him talk. I pull out and do a U-turn and drive the three blocks to the church. The same church that's been here for a century, that we've walked past since we were old enough to go uptown. Its walls are worn red brick with a red brick fence around a yard with a black wooden sign that has announcements in white letters. We line up to the big black doors under a roof like a covered porch, except it's a covered church porch that fifty people can stand under. The doors open and we parade in to find a seat.

A lineup forms to the casket which is open at the front. I can see the polished wooden lid and the soft silk pillow lining from where we sit at the back. I walk up and get in line. I don't know if Oscar and Ted are in line. The line moves step by slow step, like slaves in a cartoon. I get to Dusty and look in. He is lying with his eyes closed, his long hair on the white pillow. His moustache makes him look Mexican. I want to say get up, Dusty. Quit fucking around. But Dusty isn't moving or talking.

I head back to my seat, looking at the faces in the crowd as I make my way down the aisle. I see Westy and Rowley, the Julikers and Hans. I nod to them and to my old hockey coaches, Mr. Wade and Mr. Towns. I see lots of people I know but most are looking at their hands or their purses. The place is quiet except for rustling of clothes and soft murmurings.

Organ music begins and people stand up. I don't. They sit down again and the preacher speaks. I close my eyes. Then it's over and I do stand because the family is walking down behind the casket. I look at Mr. Dost. He looks like someone punched his face forty times. I look at Mrs. Dost. She is in a black suit and her blond hair is tucked up under a cap with a net that covers her eyes. She has a nice figure, nice shoes. And she is crying into a hankie. We all follow out of the church in a respectful order. It is so quiet. Oscar, Ted and I walk to Gibby's car and get in. We don't even speak to each other. I drive to the lake, to the graveyard. We are early so I park on the hill and we get out and stand on the hill. I am religious enough to think of the three crosses, Jesus and two thieves: Oscar, Ted and me. It strikes me as funny but I dare not crack a smile. And I am thinking if life is so fragile, fuck life. And then I think that Jesus was supposed to have survived death in some strange fashion. And that Christians are supposed to survive death too. And then I think that I could never imagine a guy like Jesus in church. He would be like the drifter guy who came through town and got in trouble for swimming naked with his dog at the number two bridge. He would laugh at the cops and ask what was wrong with being naked. The human body is God's creation. That was before they took him and his dog for a drive to Port Hope and out of Durham Region.

My mind stops when the black Cadillac hearse with the casket in the back pulls up the drive. It is followed by another black Cadillac with tinted windows.

The James Bond funeral guys in black suits with sunglasses help the Dosts out of the car. The pallbearers line up behind the hearse. And my stinking tie feels like it is made of lead, pulling my head down. They take the casket and carry it. The preacher leads the way. The family follows and then the crowd of mourners. We stay on the hill, three overseers, like crows who watch but don't participate who possess understandings beyond this event.

I had already figured out that life was a piece of shit and watching this just confirms it. The casket is beside the open hole in the dirt. The excavated mound is under AstroTurf behind the gathering crowd. Mrs. Dost is weeping and leaning on her husband. She turns and hides her face in his chest. The preacher is trying to make this acceptable with words I cannot hear. He closes the Bible and takes some dirt from the ground and throws it on the casket. The pallbearers take the green straps that are on each side to lower the casket into the ground.

"No Philip! No! Let me go. Let me go," Mrs. Dost cries and strains against Mr. Dost who has her by the waist. She reaches for the grave after the casket is below our line of sight. Mr. Dost pulls her back and hugs her to him.

"Let's get out of here," I say.

"Let's," Ted says and Oscar just follows us to the car. We get in and I start the engine and turn on the air conditioning. Ted and Oscar light up smokes. I drop the shift into drive to move away from the long line of parked cars that now line the drive. Oscar starts crying. I can hear him sobbing. Coughing, man, sobs that no one is supposed to hear. I look in the rear-view. Tears the size of raindrops are falling off his cheeks and chin. He stops after a few minutes. No one is speaking.

"You okay, Oscar?" I say, but he just stares out the window. I take Oscar home first and then Ted.

"See ya, Moose," he says.

I take the car back to Gibby's farm. My mom follows me in mine.

"How was it?" Gibby says, no longer in uniform but in jeans and T-shirt and Kodiak boots. He is beside his tractor.

"Death is weird," I answer him.

"It's hard to accept," he says.

I just nod. "Thanks for the car."

"Okay," he says and gets on the tractor and I walk over to my car and get in. I know Gibby found his father dead, hanging in a tree. My mother has moved to the passenger side and I ask her, "How old was Gibby when he found his dad?"

"He was a man, Ronnie. He may have already started on the force." I pull the shift into drive and feel a space inside myself opening, a space that must be familiar to Gibby. It is a long empty space where things continue forever. And I feel that I am trespassing, that I don't belong here. I fear that I will feel this way every day for the rest of my life.

I meet Ted after work the next day. We go for a drive in his pickup truck. It is a '68 GMC with the 283 and a three-speed shift kit on the floor. It has wide tires and the low ratio gears make it hop. And Ted loves to make it hop.

We drive east on Highway 2 to escape the scrutiny of the Durham Regional Police. We have found the OPP of

Port Hope to have a better sense of humour. We drive to a road allowance north of Welcome and pull off and stop the engine. I take out a joint and light it, take a long draw and pass it to Ted.

"Oscar quit partying," Ted says. "And he asked that girl to marry him." He takes the joint and inhales while I cough my lungs up.

"What? How did you hear that?" I ask.

"He told me. I saw him uptown. Says he doesn't need to party anymore." He passes the joint back but I just hold it and stare.

"What did his girlfriend say?"

"She said yes."

I look at Ted and then at the joint which is about to drop a coal.

"Oscar's so young to get married," I say. I knock the end off and take a toke.

"He said Dusty was too young to die."

I am looking out the windshield at a cedar clump in the middle of a field with cows grazing just beyond.

"If I thought I could be happy without partying I would go straight," I say. "But I am so fucked up." I look at Ted. "I bet a lot of people feel that way. Get married and have kids. Who would want to have kids? This is a horrible world. Everyone I know feels that way. I hope Oscar is happy. I bet he will be."

Ted puts the roach on a clip and passes it to me. I pull the telescopic arm out and put the apparatus before my lips, but before I inhale I say, "What's the Bible say? Blessed are they that mourn. Better to stay high than to cry." And I snicker and chuckle.

Ted laughs too. He scrunches his face and pulls his neck back and hushes air through his teeth when he laughs. He gets me. It is funny.

He starts the truck and we drive back to Newtonville and get two Pepsis at the General Store. He drives down to the lake and parks on a farmer's lane dead end, a set of ruts between grass. He stops and we sit and watch the lake cap like ten thousand seagulls appearing and disappearing.

"Ted," I say.

"Moose."

"This makes me happy."

"What?"

"Just sitting here watching the world. Whenever I wish for things, I get fucked up."

Ted nods and leans his head on his arm, which is braced against the side-door window frame.

"But you can't help but wish for things, can you?"

Ted inhales and exhales slowly.

"But wanting things fucks you up, because as soon as you want it you realize you don't have what you want. And even when you get what you want you still want more. So it never ends. That's what Millson says."

He looks sideways at me. "What does Millson say?"

"Life is a spin. You just keep spinning through things and every time you spin deeper into them. And that is all you will do all your life."

Ted snickers through his nose. I get out of the truck and walk toward the lake. There is a small rise and the wind off the water is cool. I lie down in the grass and look up at the clouds drifting over in white puffs. And someone is kicking my side.

12

"Wake up, Moose."

I look up and Zietz and Mike and Gomes are looking down, three heads in a symmetrical circle with the blue sky between them. They all laugh at me. Just for a moment I know I was dreaming a reality. I was there at that funeral. But the thought is like one of those streamers I see in front of my eyes: turn your head and it's gone.

"Wow, man. Were you gone!" Gomes says.

"Let's get breakfast," Mike adds as I stand up.

We get in the car. Mike is in front with me. We drive the service road to the next ramp where there is a McDonald's. Inside, we line up for the big breakfast and Gomes gets a newspaper. On the front is the headline "Riot," and a picture of the stage at the concert.

"That wasn't a riot," Zietz says. "That was a great concert."

We find a table with a view of the highway. I peel the lid of my Styrofoam container to see the rich yellow of food-coloured eggs and bacon which looks like it has been ironed instead of fried. There is a pancake and a hash brown. The hash brown is the most appealing and I douse it with salt and take a mouthful. I take the plastic container of syrup and peel off the lid and pour the contents over everything.

"You know that this stuff is processed cardboard," I say. Mike laughs.

"I loved the end when he was jumping through the air," Zietz says, smiling and nodding at us in turn.

"Yeah, man," Gomes says, leaning back and running his fingers through his hair. "He's insane."

"But he sure could dodge those bottles and shoes," I say. "But why throw stuff at him?" I am shaking my head and looking around at the guys.

"That's probably why they didn't do an encore. Throw bottles at me, fuck you." Zietz completes his comment with a middle finger thrust.

"Keep it down, Zietz. There's kids around," Mike says, looking at a little boy who's looking at us with wide eyes and open mouth.

"They never do encores," Gomes adds, ignoring the Mike comment and the kid. "The crowd goes nuts and they see how long and when it starts to die down the lights come on."

"Or the roadies come out," Zietz says.

"Jagger looked buzzed," I say.

Mike laughs. "A few times he ran from the front like he forgot where he was."

"This breakfast sucks," I say, throwing the plastic utensils into the food and closing the lid. I stand and so do the others, taking the food with them to the trash.

"Let me finish," Zietz says, hurrying his consumption.

"Bring it with ya, Zietz," I say.

"Nah, you're right," he says. "This tastes like shit."

We walk out in a line that makes me think of John, Paul, George and Ringo, except it's me, Mike, Gomes and Zietz. "It's going to be hot," I say.

"Get rid of the chicken, Moose."

"Good idea, Zietz." I pop the trunk, take the cooler to a concrete garbage bin and empty the contents while turning my head away. "When I get home I'm going to get a two-four and go to the duck pond." I put the lid on the cooler and put it back.

"I'm with you," Gomes says.

"I gotta work, Moose," Zietz says.

"I have to go home too," Mike says.

"Can you feel the leash?" I say to Mike as I get in the car. He doesn't say anything. Sometimes I think Mike is with his girl because it's his destiny. Like they had planned being together before they were born. But sometimes I don't think he likes it. Maybe getting laid isn't all it's cracked up to be.

"I'll have to stop in home," I say to Gomes as I start up the engine. "Just to show them I'm alive and wasn't killed in the riot."

Gomes asks from the back as I pull out of the ramp, "Do you think your old man will be pissed, Moose?"

"Yeah. I think when he sees the scrape down the side of the car he'll freak out." But I am remembering Dusty's parents and I become quiet for a moment. I accelerate onto the QEW and look in the rear-view at Gomes. "Remember the hash?"

"What happened?" Mike asks with a smile and glassy eyes. He knows my old man from hockey. Dad was our coach for a while.

"My parents have gone to a friend's cottage for the weekend. I have this quarter of hash and I go get Gomes and we make up one of those paper-towel-roll pipes—cut a hole in it, get some foil and push it in to make a bowl and pierce it with a fork. We made that up and stood in the kitchen and smoked the hash. We got ripped and decided that we would go uptown for a Pepsi. So we leave the hash and the pipe and a pack of tobacco on the table and go uptown. We head uptown, and on the way back, just at the old-age home, we look across and the car is in the driveway."

"This car," Gomes says.

"Yes, at that time it was still Dad's car. I said to Gomes, You go, man. But he says no way, man, I'm going in with you. So we cross and go into the house. The hash we had left on the table is gone. The tobacco is gone. The only thing left is the stupid paper-towel-roll pipe sitting on the table with my old man sitting at the end. He says to Gomes, Thanks, Sam. You can leave. So Gomes leaves and I sit down for the thousandth lecture on dope and its evil effects. But then I ask him about his friends at GM who do dope and the lectures become stories."

"But what about the time your brakes were grinding?" Gomes asks. "We went in the house and Moose told his old man that the car was making a noise and his father took it for a drive and came back. He jumped out of the car and stomped to the deck. We were all just sitting there. It's the brakes. It's the goddamn brakes! I've never seen anyone as mad as you, Moose. I thought you two were going to fight."

"He gave me the car. It was his big deal. That car meant everything to him. He would spend all afternoon under the hood tuning the carb. He wanted me to care about the car the way he did. But I don't give a fuck about the car. It just gets me around. And what do I know about brakes. I had to park the car until we did the brakes together. More lectures on car maintenance." We are all laughing. "Listen," I say, "he gets that energy going, man. When he revs up, no one messes with him. I have this uncle, a biker, a huge guy. He fought Spider at the Elmhurst."

"I remember that," Zietz interrupts.

"Yeah," I continue. "He dinnered Spider. Not many people could do that. So the whole family is at this party at my uncle's parents in Oshawa. They have a cherry tree and a pool shaped like a kidney bean. My cousin Kevin and I go to get some stuff at the store and we come back and my other cousin meets us in the driveway. You won't believe what happened, he says. Uncle Greg, that's the biker, tried to pick up Uncle Ron and throw him in the pool. He grabbed him around the waist like this—he was showing us how—and tries to carry him to the pool. But Uncle Ron hooks his legs around Uncle Greg's and straightens his back and pulls his legs forward and trips Uncle Greg. And then he pins Uncle Greg and makes him say give."

We are all laughing.

"I can see that," Mike says. "Remember when he would pace the boards at the rink? The time you threw your stick from centre ice into the penalty box? Nobody could believe it. And he came running down the boards to hang his head around the partition to give you shit. Nobody could believe you two."

I am smiling, dropping into reverie. The lanes widen as we get on the Gardiner. "He was better as a coach," I say.

"He was a good coach," Mike agrees.

"Yeah. We had some good times driving to games together. We'd talk about all kinds of shit. He's a good guy, you know."

"Just a little crazy, like you, Moose," Gomes says from the back.

"I think all dads are a little insane," Mike says.

"For sure," I answer and push in the Beatles.

Eleanor Rigby comes on. McCartney singing. I hear snoring from the back seat. Zietz is sleeping. Everyone else is quiet, watching out the windows as we cruise below Toronto and over the islands and the lake, past the tall shiny buildings and the old sugar silos.

"It's new on one side and old on the other," Gomes says.

We head north on the Don Valley, up alongside the river which I can see now and then, scummy and slow and green. The trees are thick and rise with the hills, hiding big houses I can barely see. Then we hit the 401 and gas it toward home. The car is smooth and has lots of power. I look in the rear-view and Gomes is asleep too. Mike and I listen on, sitting in the front. Yellow Submarine is playing and we sing it together. I enjoy this camaraderie after a major drug binge, when we've all stretched our minds like kids' balloons at a party and we are just returning to normal.

I hit Oshawa and pass the sprawling GM plant on the right and Mike who works there looks askance and says, "Shithole."

I laugh. I didn't get hired even though I applied. My grandfather was the president of the union. My dad and all my uncles work there. All my cousins got jobs and some of them are more fucked up than I am. Someone blackballed me and I am certain it was my old man.

"I don't want you working in the plant," he used to say, in the same gruff tone he would say other things, like "never use a woman" and "never walk away from a fight." And even though it is a shithole, like Mike said, the pay is good and it's a steady job which is not easy to come by.

"My old man's ashamed of me," I say. "That's why I never got in."

Mike nods. He knows what I am talking about. "What are you going to do?" he asks.

"Wind up working in a gas station." We both laugh because it's a Frank Zappa song. Mike and I went to the Gardens to see Zappa. It was amazing. So amazing we never could explain what made it so amazing to anyone but ourselves.

The laughter subsides into quiet. We pass Liberty Street in Bowmanville. Familiar fields come into view along with farms of families we know until the Ceresdale Fertilizer tower heralds Newcastle and the exit for Mill Street. I hug the ramp and exit a little too fast with a soft squeal of tire. The cop station is across from us when I stop at the stop sign. Gibby the cop works there. I think of Dusty and his funeral. How Gibby lent us his car. I think of Oscar and Ted.

"Hey Gibby!" Mike waves at the cop shop. Mike and I worked together at Gibson's Orchard when we were younger.

"A good guy," I say. Mike laughs. I look at him. He has long black hair and looks like a cross between Jim Morrison and Paul McCartney.

"Go!" he says, pointing ahead.

I drive north on Mill, past my house and the four corners and out to the third line. Zietz and Gomes awaken, but are quiet and rubbing their eyes like three-year-olds just up from a nap.

"Are we home?" Zietz asks.

I pull in Mike's driveway. His Trans Am is parked. Another benefit of working in GM, being able to afford a nice car. I pop the trunk and Mike gets out, grabs his stuff and closes the trunk lid.

"Thanks, Ron," he says and waves while Gomes crawls out and gets in the front. I back out and head east toward Newtonville. The car is as quiet as the hum of the wheels on the asphalt. I head down to Highway 2 and turn in Zietz's drive. I get out to help him get his tent and stuff.

"Thanks, Moose," he says and walks to his house.

"I call ya, Zietz," Gomes says and Zietz answers with the backward palm wave.

Gomes and I head back to town. I turn left at the four corners and south toward my house. I turn on Robert Street and into my own driveway. Mom and Dad are on the deck waiting. Dad in no shirt and his work pants, leaning on the railing, and Mom in slacks and top sitting in a lawn chair. They both stand and Dad puts his hand around her, resting it on her hip. I see he is looking at the car dent. I get out and so does Gomes.

"Did you have a good time?" Dad asks in a cheerful voice.

I look at Gomes, raise an eyebrow and shrug.

"Yeah. It was amazing. Best concert ever," I answer.

"We were worried," Mom says. "We saw the riot on TV."

Gomes and I break into laughs. "There was no riot," I say. "There were ninety thousand people at that concert and at the end a few hundred stood around whining and rushing the stage."

But they both just stand there smiling. "We are just happy you're home safe." Mom grips Dad's hand at her waist.

I look into his eyes and then into hers. I have never seen this before. It's love. It's adoration. It's bigger than them. I am thinking it must always have been there but I never noticed. I look at the ground. I look at them. It's still there, coming through. I look back at the ground.

13

"We are going to go to the duck pond for a swim," I say.

"Okay, son," Dad says. "Will you be home for dinner?"

"Yeah, I will," I say. "I'll take a nap before going in tonight."

Gomes and I get back in the car and I back out the driveway. We go uptown and buy a two-four of Export Ale. Then to Becker's to buy a bag of ice. On the main street I open the trunk and drop the bag of ice on the pavement to break it up. I fill the bottom of the cooler with the cubes of cold and I think, This is the chicken cooler. Will I get sick? The cooler only takes half the case and I fold the cardboard flaps and push the beer back into the recesses of the trunk. I pour the rest of the ice over the bottles, put the lid on and close the trunk.

Gomes, who has been standing and watching, smiles a wide grin.

"Ice-cold Ex," he says as we get in the car and pull a U-turn and head toward Kendal.

"You got a joint?" I ask Gomes. He pulls one out, lights it and we pass and toke as we criss and cross the backroads, dust billowing behind us and the Beatles blaring out the windows.

We get to the duck pond, a conservation area with a green pond surrounded by short willow shrubs and picnic sites. We park down by the small sand beach and take a picnic table and carry it out into the pond. It floats slowly away. I get the cooler from the trunk and put it in the water and it floats. I push it out to follow the picnic table into the sunshine. We sit at that table, sunk up to our ribs in the coolish wet. I reach and pull the cooler to us and remove the lid. The beers are freezing to the touch and Sam procures an opener from his pocket and lifts the caps from the bottles I pass to him.

"Cold beer, cool water, hot day," Gomes says.

We sit and drink, look around. We don't say much. We are good at this. Friends don't need to talk. And Gomes and I are good friends. After four beers I get off and swim to shore, grab another picnic table and pull it into the water. The planked top is level with the water's surface. I pull myself up on top and turn on my back with my face to the sun. The rays impregnate my body with heat.

And there is a dog licking my face. I look up at a square-headed black Lab. "Drum, Drum!" I hear a woman's voice calling. I realize that I am cold and that I have thick clothing on, a sweater and jeans, and I am in a yellowed marsh in the fall, sitting beside a stream in bare feet. My boots and socks are beside my feet and the dog is pushing me with his body, wrestling with me. I grab his neck and wrestle him down. I am laughing at his comic energy, relentlessly grabbing my arms and hands with his soft mouth, the teeth a light pressure into my bones. I get up and see the woman, red hair sticking out of a hunter's plaid cap and wide sunglasses that hide most of her upper face, but she has a small mouth and chin.

Otherwise she is dressed as I am, in sweater, boots and jeans.

"Patsy?" I say.

I suddenly remember Sunderland and that I am middle-aged and journeying again, stopping the world and diving in between the shades of my life. I shake my head and she comes and pulls the dog back. I take the opportunity to pull on my socks and boots.

"Are you all right?" the woman asks me.

"Yeah, thanks," I say, getting to my feet.

The dog is now on a leash but still straining to get to me.

"I once had a dog named Drum," I say.

"Yes, he obviously knows you," she says.

"Pardon me?" I ask, but she is looking down and patting the dog's head. "Do I know you?"

"We must be off. We need to burn off this youthful energy. Don't we, Drum?" She looks up at me. "He loves the marsh. Memories of the good old days of duck hunting."

I just nod. "'Bye," she says and moves down the path.

Things are getting strange. I had a dog named Drum, a black Lab just like that when I was a teenager and I had a girlfriend just like that when I was a little older.

And they are very similar to the dog and lady that just left me. Can people detach from their lives with you and enter into your experience in a completely different way? That would mean they can affect your life, that they can change you without you wanting them to. If that was Patsy and Drum, they have changed me. Even thinking that they might be Patsy and Drum has changed me.

I see my bike and remember riding here. I go and lift it out of the grass, get on and pedal home, past the Co-op and the grain elevator, past the four corners and up the hill to my old house. I will be happy to see my wife. She says this house winks and it does. It is missing a window on the west side of the front door, closed up when they moved the stairs a long time ago. So it has one window on the east side, the door and a blank wall on the west and it does seem out of balance, like a wink.

They say this house is haunted, and my wife has seen a ball of energy in her closet. It hovered for a moment before her and then whizzed past. I wonder if this house is part of the plan to be doing what I am doing. I park my bike and go inside. No one is home. But it all becomes familiar. I am thinking that this stopping the world and time travel may become dangerous.

PART TWO

14

Well hello, it's me. I hafta laugh at that. The old Todd Rundgren song. I remember him on TV in a body suit with a big boner stretching down along his leg, singing and playing his piano. Some artists stay with you. I listened to the Stones all through my life, watched the videos over and over. There is a YouTube video of the Some Girls tour in '78. It revives memories to watch them. I read Keith Richards' biography and he said they were at their best on that tour. He had cleaned up from heroin for good and the band was new and fresh. Plus, the punk rock scene had inspired a new raunchiness in the band. And that is what we witnessed all those years ago. In many ways, it still defines me.

In many ways it was the Stones, especially Mick Jagger, who created my younger middle-aged transcendentalist self who discovered how to stop the world. The Stones concert of '78 never died but grew with me into my forties and fifties. Like a cyclone of dissatisfaction, it turned and distorted me into someone different, a stand-out from the crowd. I remember that time in my life with fondness. It was when I stopped being a nice guy. Hey, I was always and still am a nice guy but I kept my mouth shut too often. I was overweight and drank too much, beer especially, but (and I remember writing this, for as I am writing it now, I am writing it then) I became what could be termed an outspoken person. Not that I would blather on about bullshit but I became an economist of words and liquor and food. If someone was talking shit I would speak, quietly and with authority but effectively. Like a Sugar Ray Leonard jab, setting up the powerhouse which I seldom delivered, because as soon as you contradict a loudmouth they get louder and stupider. I love that word, loudmouth. It has survived in my vocabulary from my childhood. But nonetheless I became known for my brash opinions. Not that I was a know-it-all. But I gained the understanding that we are eternal beings with a goal to escape the never-ending boredom of lives repeating. Over and over again, the same stupid themes being played out, the incessant rhythm of the human psyche, drama, drama, drama.

Oh yes, stopping time. I should talk about that. It's a lot like dreaming. Because dreaming is all about energy and energy is all about creating reality. Dreams are reality, folks. You should know that. Right now transcendental man is dreaming me at this creek. The fall is full-on and the leaves litter the black water like a skin. Like Perelandra, the Lewis book where Ransom is on Venus and there are islands that float like hides on the ocean. Lewis created that world with his dreaming. That world exists, as does Middle Earth, as does Frolix 8 and the aliens that came with Thors Provoni. I have travelled to these places. I have met Thors Provoni and Ransom. I have met Gandalf and Frodo. Elves do exist. And if you believe in them, they appear.

I have travelled to places you could never imagine, but someone imagined them and they exist. You see, I am here because the dreamer is dreaming me. He is not just thinking about me. He is dreaming me.

Dreaming is different from thinking. When you dream you let yourself go with your thoughts. Your imagination becomes you; it carries you. Everyone does this. It's just that no one believes it. When you believe in your dreams you vanish into them.

There is a book by Auster called Travels in the Scriptorium. His characters from all his novels got together and dreamed a world. And then they kidnapped him into it and dreamed him as an old man with Alzheimer's Disease.

He remembers little bits of who they are and is treated kindly by some and with hostility by others. But he is their creator. This they all know. Without him they do not exist and they now have a whole eternity to create their own lives, their own realities.

The earth is like that. Jehovah is just one of the sick puppies that created this place. The Greek gods were real and still are, although the world they inhabit now is a piece of shit. We are the descendants of such so-called gods, and you could argue that this world is also a piece of shit. But it's good, isn't it? I mean, living is good fun, and if you realize you are an eternal being it is even better. I wrote a book about a boy named Cash. His journey was to discover the worlds he created, and in spite of all the crazy shit he invented it was still a great place to be. I wrote that book from here, you know. I wrote it backwards in time. I had to help my younger idealist and he came through just fine.

There is an owl in the bush. It is the same one that I heard a long time ago sitting around a pond in a nature sanctuary. How do I know? That owl is my spirit guide. I have only heard him a dozen times. I have only seen him twice. The first was when I was driving in my old Chev station wagon. There were the Rowleys, Robert Towns and me. I was just old enough to have a licence. Towns was a hunter and fisherman and a real outdoors guy while still being a real freak. He was a skinny guy with Rod Stewart hair and eyes that always seemed to vibrate in his head.

"Stop!" Towns said as I drove down the 4th Concession north of town, past a marsh with stumps standing twenty feet tall.

"What?" I said to Towns. I didn't like him very much. But I liked his old man so I tolerated him.

"An owl! I saw a fucking owl!"

So I backed up the road while Towns hung his head out the window in the summer dust that plumed off the tires.

"There, there, there," he pointed.

We all got out, all four of us, and looked to where he was pointing and sure enough, there was a massive bird, thick like a stump, grey and blue with the true kaleidoscope eyes. He turned his head and extended it up and down like a mechanism, not like something living. He was over half as tall as me and I bet he weighed fifty pounds. I saw a rock the size of my fist arc in the air, directly in line with the bird.

"Fuck, Towns!" I said and went to grab him but the bird just lifted his body with his thick wings, like feather-covered ironing boards, each as long as my arm. I was in awe as Towns launched another. The bird just lifted out of the way.

"Don't throw another one, Towns, or I'll throw you."

He listened and stopped. We watched the owl and he watched us, stretching his neck and twisting his head, blinking one beady eye and then the other, lifting his appendages to swat the air and then settling. Then he lifted off the stump he had been sitting on and glided through the marsh, flying perpendicular and then flat and then the opposite perpendicular, through the densest bush like a god, like a graceful spirit. And then he was gone.

But he is here. Now he comes every night. He bounces his high-pitched sound bubbles across the water to me. Such magic soothes me and keeps me sane.

Everything here is sounds and smells of decay. Limbs of trees dropping in the forest, and the air is a little septic. I don't know how long I have been here. The coyotes come around at night. Aliens yipping and yowling like they are raising an ecstatic spirit to dance for me. I walked downstream to some clear faster water yesterday and caught a red-tail sucker. I had to throw it back, of course. You can't eat suckers in the fall. I remember catching one in the springtime, when I was just a kid, maybe seven or eight years old, with my dad and mom. The water in this creek was turbulent and fast, green and muddy grey, like swirls of chocolate in mint, and the fish jumped out of the water two feet in the air. And it was big, over five pounds. We gave it to an old guy who witnessed the whole thing.

"You eat them?" my kid self asked the old man.

"You can eat them in the spring," Dad answered on behalf of the old man.

These memories are comforting. *Recapitulation* is what it is called. Recapitulation is reliving your life from a detached perspective. Living everything over again to release the emotional energy to the eagle. Because the eagle eats that energy and if you have it in you when you die the eagle eats you. Well, maybe not all of you, but a lot of you. But if you get rid of all of the human emotional attachments before your death, you can sail past the eagle into the unknown. To explore brave new worlds. Isn't that what James T. Kirk said?

But it's true. At this stage of the game, at the end of my life, attaining detachment is easier. It's still hard. I still have loves. I love my daughter, my grandson, my wife, my old friend Zietz. But this tumour in my side gave me fair warning. I staged the party, a lot like Bilbo Baggins, but I don't have a ring.

So I am telling the story for a while. I have stopped time for so long now that I can move about with ease. As easy as you can conjure a memory, I conjure a past and step into it.

Women memories are the most troublesome. They drag at me like a ball and chain, like being tethered to a tree. My life was always surrounded by the opposite sex. I lived in a house that took in wives, daughters, mothers-in-law, nieces, women friends who had no home. In the writers' groups, guys were outnumbered five to one, ten to one, usually just me and women. I rode horses and most of the time I was the only male rider in the barn. Over the years women have been my closest friends and my bitterest foes. I had intimate confidants whom I fell for. I never had affairs, primarily because I never wanted to create turmoil in another person, especially a person I cared for.

But I did fall in love. And when you fall in love you create soul ties and soul ties are eternal and they bind you to this earth. In fact, all relationships are eternal. They go on forever and ever. It's the same cast appearing as different characters. I don't know who we really are. I don't know if we stage these dramas ourselves. But I don't think so. I think it is more random than that. I think it is more impersonal than that. I think it is like a jelly mould that we swim around in until we discover that the jelly can be moulded with our thoughts, beliefs and intentions. I am hoping to discover this for certain as I recapitulate my life, as I gain freedom from the random.

Yes, relationships are eternal and eternally morphing. I once said this to a friend who is a bit mad to begin with. But we are all a bit mad. One of the funniest trips I have ever made was to Philip K. Dick's Alphane Moon. A place where all the mental disorders are formed into different cities. The Pares, the Manses and the Schitzs, the Heebs, the Polys, the Deps, all have their own distinct interpretation of the world and have created their towns accordingly.

But my friend is an ObCom. He has an obsessive-compulsive disorder and when I told him all relationships are eternal, he gasped. Gotcha! You see, we are so many selves. Like we are a billion cells, we are also a billion selves, all going off in different directions. Bits of you and me running free. Don't be dismayed. It is how the game is played.

Ha-ha! I am a crazy old man in the bush. Don't worry. Many of the selves you are living are happy and contented people. (You don't become dogs or cats. That option is never open to you.) Actually, it's about fifty percent of you that lives the happy dream, the lotto dream, while the other fifty percent lives the contrast that produces the dream. And here's the thing. The grand consciousness, what you would call the real you, likes to hang around the contrast. It enjoys the shit storm, in greater or lesser degrees.

I admit we like the relief. But from where you are you can choose to go deeper into the shit and you quite often do. I've done that too. Where hatred turns into murder. Yes, friend. I have murdered people in my dreams—which is reality, as you now know. And I have gone with my murdering self into the darkness. Don't judge, you are a rapist. You have been raped. You have been murdered. We have all tried on the coats and hats. Remember the Bugs Bunny cartoon, the truck full of hats that lost its load into the wind, hats landing on Bugs and Daffy, totally changing their personas? We all try on lives for a while, to see how they fit. But relax, I intend to stay within the extension of the life, or lives of this guy, me, Moose.

Whoa! I have just been joined by my cousin, Kevin Kennelly. Kevin is dead but death does not exist. Kev was like my big brother in real life. He is laughing and shaking his head.

"Is death more real than life, Kev?"

Now he is nodding. "More real, Ronnie."

Ronnie is what Kevin calls me. Because my dad's name was Ron everyone in the family called me Ronnie.

"Or Potter," Kev adds. "Because I assume we are going to Whitney."

"Yes, that was the plan," I say.

"And Patsy called you Potter."

"Yes, she did," I say.

"Did she ever call you by your first name?"

I am laughing. "Nope. I was just Potter. I saw her at the Beaver River with my old dog Drum. I was in my fifties. I was sure it was her but she was fucking with my head. I had just re-emerged from some mind trip. Can people enter your experience like that?"

I look at Kev. He is a seventeen-year-old. Long straight hair combed off one side with a part. He has small eyes close together like mine and an oversized schnoz and a body with a barrel chest and short legs. He is wearing a muscle shirt and jeans and Kodiaks. Just what we wore that summer. He ignores my question completely.

"I like it here," he says. "Remember Grandma brought us here? All of us: you, me, your brother Rob, my brothers and my sister Cathy. We walked down this path. We stood on that bridge."

Kev and I spent a lot of time here when we were kids. I am talking of the farmhouse I passed on the way in, the old log cabin built in the early 1800s. We would build rafts out of cedar rails and old doors, search for old bottles in the barn and along the fence lines, and spy on the Pitt girls who lived down the road.

"Remember when you and I got lost?" I ask him.

"How old were you, Ronnie? Maybe six or seven. And you freaked out because you saw a no trespassing sign and were afraid we would be arrested."

"And I ran, I ran into the marsh and you ran and caught me and carried me on your shoulders through all that water."

"And it was freezing because it was spring and the snow had just melted."

"And the adults came looking for us," I say slowly because I can see them. My dad and Kev's dad, Uncle Bob and Mom and Aunt Beth.

Kev is laughing but I am crying, weeping gently with my chin on my old chest.

"Nobody's dead, Ronnie. You will see them all again."

"And what are you here for?" I ask, looking up and reaching to stir the fire. The coals under the sticks are red and yellow hot. I reach and throw two more sticks on top.

"You know how you talk of parallel lives? I am here to help you experience one." I can feel my body changing. I was fourteen the summer we went to Whitney. I was fourteen but looked twenty. I could walk in for booze in any town, in any bar. Kev was seventeen, as I said, but we both looked older.

"I've seen myself, you know. I saw myself at a Rolling Stones concert. And I've seen myself as an old man from my younger self. I can do it here by the fire when I'm alone. But they weren't parallel lives. They were this life at various stages, like time travel."

"I've seen myself too," Kev adds. "Once I bought gas from myself. I was in the kiosk and this big black Harley pulls in, all chrome and loud. He pulls in, all attitude, black leathers, black helmet, black gloves and tall boots. The Eagles were playing in the shed, the greatest hits. I remember Desperado, because I thought to myself, This guy is a desperado. He was a big guy and he struggled to push himself off the bike. He got off and hiked his belt under his big gut."

Kev interrupts his narrative with snorts of laughter.

"He took off his helmet and I can see from the back he has an old-guy wrinkled neck and an old-guy bald head, warts and all."

I laugh because I know the old Cromwell quote. "Paint me warts and all," I say.

Kev winks and smiles on the verge of a guffaw. He continues.

"So he takes the nozzle and flips the gas cap open on the top of the tank. And like all bikers he fills his own tank."

I nod. "Yeah, yeah. They do that."

Kev looks at me. "And then I walk around to face him and it's me."

"What were you doing? I mean the biker you."

"Laughing," Kev says. "Laughing at myself."

"And what did you make of that?" I ask but I already know the answer because every time my old-man self has turned up he has had the same message, delivered in some comic fashion.

"I was laughing," Kev said. "Laughing at myself. I mean older me was laughing at younger me. Like our uncles used to laugh at us."

"When we took ourselves too seriously," I say. "But don't let me interrupt. What did younger you, Whitney you, make of it?"

"It scared me, Ronnie. It was like this older me had found some secret, some devilish secret." He stoops and leans toward me and winks again. "He follows me around. I bet he's here."

"No one's here, Kev. It's just you and me and you're dead."

He looks at me and nods, leans back. "Yeah, sure. But it scared the hell out of me. I was a Catholic and I took those things seriously. I believed in the Mass and here I am an old fat guy, probably in my fifties, mocking myself. That's what it felt like. I thought the devil was playing a mean trick. That's what I concluded."

"What do you think now?" I stand and stir the fire and stoop to let the radiant heat wash my face and arms and chest.

"It was over so fast," Kev continues. "He paid me cash, got on his bike and burned out of there. Then I set out to convince myself it never really happened. I did not want to believe in what had happened. But not long before I died I took a trip on the Harley. I had forgotten all about the incident. I came here to the gas station and everything had changed, but this kid came out to serve me, and Ronnie, it was me. And I looked up and there was the old Texaco star hanging from that post, and the old prefab house was there and the propane tank and the canoes stacked against the retaining wall. I was here, Ronnie. I had slipped back in time but it was not real time. It was like a time between times. When you are present with yourself, when two of you are in the same place at the same time, that's parallel."

I look around and instead of being in the bush by my tent we are sitting in the Shell station restaurant beside the Madawaska River where Highway 60 passes over it. I look at Kev and laugh, slap my knee and say, "Holy shit! You're just a kid." Which in fact he's not. He's seventeen years old and I assume I am his fourteen-year-old counterpart.

Anne comes over in an apron to take our order. She is blond, green-eyed, perfectly proportioned and the object of desire for every kid between sixteen and twenty-five for at least a sixty-mile radius. She smiles like she has been smiling for decades, trapped in a hologram, smiling Anne.

I look at Kev. His eyes sparkle like a demon, like a sorcerer who has played me into a trap.

"Bacon, eggs, brown toast and coffee for both of us, please," I say.

"What's wrong with Kevin?" Anne says. "Cat got his tongue?"

"Nah, he drove home last night. Just got back. Pulled an all-nighter."

She stoops and looks at Kev's eyes. He just keeps looking at me.

"Looks to me like he had some help keeping awake," Anne says and smiles and walks away.

Kev snickers. "I love this, Ronnie, turning up places in your life. It never gets boring."

I nod, look away, think about the unknown. Kev, as if he reads thoughts, says, "There is still a lot of the unknown here. You can explore forever."

And that gets a smile out of me.

We eat our breakfast while looking around. Across the road is Arnold's Chicken, which has a pool hall and is where we met most of the locals, Chub and Choog, Goose and his brother Brad, Albert and Raymond. It's also where we met Patsy and Bonnie, two sisters: Patsy, short with red hair and green eyes, a compact version of Wilma Flintstone, and Bonnie, tall with black hair and black eyes and Indian, kinda like Betty. How they were sisters I never figured. They had brothers also but I never figured out who were brothers and who were cousins and why we never got to see the parents because I was always at their house.

"Do you remember the first day we were here and we canoed up from the lake to the bridge?" Kev says while looking down at the water.

"Yes. Goose and Albert and Raymond swam up and tipped the canoe. I couldn't believe it. Who were these kids? They didn't even know us." But I am looking at the truck in the parking area. I've just seen it.

"Kev. There's the truck," I say.

"I know, Ronnie. I knew it was there."

I stand up to take a better look. It is a green '68 Ford F100 half ton with Bondo-brown fenders. I go back in my memory. Inside the cab is a bench seat with rips and holes where foam is exposed and a hard green plastic steering wheel with a chrome ring and a Ford crest for the horn and a three on the tree shifter. I sit back down and take a sip of coffee.

"Straight six, 240 cubic inches, which will never die," I say, laughing and looking out again.

"Like us, Ronnie. We will never die," Kev says with the eyes that empty into eternity.

Anne brings our breakfast and we dip toast in yolks, crunch crisp bacon and wash it down with coffees. We both finish at the same time. I watch Kev wipe his mouth with a napkin.

"Your fucking eyes kinda creep me out, man."

"Yours are the same, Ronnie. You have sunglasses on or Anne would have said the same about you."

I feel my face. "Oh yeah, I do. You should get some."

"I have some in the truck. C'mon, we should go."

We leave the cash on the table and get up and head out the glass door. The sun is hot and the air is clean with the smell of oxygenated water.

"It's the rapids," Kev says. "We never noticed then but this town has the healthiest air of anywhere."

I walk across the street and stand on the bridge. The Madawaska is slowing from the churning rapids just out of sight. I can hear them, a muffled torrent. We go swimming there every morning, jumping in the water and letting the current carry us over the rock and throwing us into the pools.

I hear the truck start and I see the dog Laddie sitting up in the back looking at me. He is emotionless, the only dog ever without emotion. He looks at me as if to say, We are waiting. He is a Collie, of course, and Kev got him from a pound and brought him to stay with him for the summer.

As I approach him he lies down in the bed of the pickup. I get in the truck passenger door and pull it shut.

"Laddie?" I say.

"This is a recreation, Ronnie. It's like a hologram that we are projecting. Everything that we remember being here will be here. We get to play with what we were before. But it always gets out of hand. Life always gets out of hand." Kev laughs.

"Do you know what's going to happen? I mean, can you remember?"

Kev looks at me sideways, quizzically. "No. No one remembers anything, Ronnie. Memory is not memory. It is recreation, always. What we are doing is stepping into what our memories have created. Everything always creates and keeps on creating. Memories are thoughts and thoughts create other thoughts and then they bundle together and form worlds. And those worlds form beings. But you already know that. I've read your books. You've been to the worlds that writers have created. But this is your world that you created."

"Yeah, yeah. I get ya. I just didn't really believe myself. You being here makes me believe all that crap I wrote. I thought I was just recapitulating. It seemed real enough. But not as real as this."

"Listen," Kev says, "by visiting you I have hooked up with worlds I could not have imagined. And they will overlap with this one. I don't know what to expect. I can't imagine what we will find at that gas station. I have a gut instinct that we might be in a compromised situation."

"How do you mean?" I ask.

"I can't say. But we will find out."

Kev reaches his right hand down to lift the shifter and pushes in the clutch. The truck rolls back as the clutch catches. He reverses around the parking lot and then drops the shift down into low, all the while pumping the clutch and pressing the gas. We accelerate west as Kev pushes the gears up into second and down again into third.

"No seatbelts," I say.

"No fucking seatbelts," Kev affirms.

We round the bend and I see the road that slopes up toward the OPP station. Patsy and Bonnie's house is just out of sight on the same road.

"That's them," I say.

"Uh-huh," Kev says. "The scene of the big fight where you beat up Patsy's boyfriend."

"I guess you're going to be there this time."

"Wouldn't miss it for the world," Kev laughs.

"Where were you the first time?" I ask.

"I went home to Oshawa for the weekend and got laid."

I laugh and slap the foam-padded vinyl-covered steel dashboard. "Catholics are hypocrites. That's what never happened to me. I just got to punch a guy out but he was the one that ended up getting laid."

"Ah, but you got the glory, Ronnie."

I smile and look out at the town disappearing into brush, marsh and pine trees.

"At the time that was all that mattered."

"You had something to prove?" Kev asks.

"Yup, had to be a hero."

Kev laughs. "Well, you accomplished that. You became a hero. You will see things differently this time."

16

We round the bend and see it, the Texaco star with the green T in the middle, hanging from an arm off a pole, and the shed with the window looking out on the pumps, and the propane tank with the scales for filling cylinders, and the prefab cottage with no windows or doors.

"Can you believe it?" I ask Kev.

"Look," he says. "There's the truck."

Sure enough, it's the truck we are driving, an identical truck, parked in the lane that curves up behind the propane tank to the cabin. Kev pulls over to the shoulder.

"This is getting weird," I say and look over at the gas station. Two guys step down out of the cottage.

"They are us," Kev says. "And they are looking at us."

Sure enough, the two guys have stopped and are now looking at us.

"Did you ever see that show Dead Like Me?" I ask Kev.

"No. What is the relevance?" Kev is laughing.

"The people are reapers. And the thing is, they need to touch people to reclaim their souls before the people die. That way the soul is not in the body when the body gets killed. Most of the time the people are killed in some dramatic way."

"Are we reapers? Is that what you are saying, Ronnie?"

"No. But the reapers are dead already and this is their assignment in the afterlife. But this is the point. The reapers can go and see people that are alive and the one chick, the star, keeps going to see her family but they never see her as herself. They see her in another form."

I look across the road at the two guys who are us, staring at us and talking. Obviously about us.

"They don't see themselves sitting in this truck. They see two guys that aren't familiar at all. And I bet this truck does not look at all like that one parked over there."

Kev drops the shift into low and does a U-turn and pulls up to the pumps. And Kev number one walks up to the window.

"Hi. Fill it up?"

Kev says in return, "Do you take Visa?"

"For sure," Kev 1 answers and undoes the gas cap that is on the driver's side just behind Kev's shoulder.

I am looking at Ronnie 1 who is just standing by the ice cooler with a Coke in hand. I get out of the truck and walk over to him.

"Nice day," I say to start a conversation.

"That's one helluva nice truck," he answers.

"Thanks," I say. "But it's not mine, it's my cousin's, the guy driving."

"Can I look under the hood?" Ronnie 1 asks and starts walking toward the truck.

"Sure, be my guest."

Laddie sits up as we walk over.

"Those Golden Retrievers are nice dogs," Ronnie 1 says.

He walks around the front and pulls the catch and the hood lifts enough for him to reach under and lift it all the way over his head.

"Fuuuck," he says with a drawn-out vowel. "Kev, come look at this."

Kev 1 walks around and looks with Ronnie 1 under the hood.

"It's a fuckin' 390, Kev. This thing will fucking dance."

Kev comes around beside me and looks. All I can see is the old straight six all covered in oil-saturated grime.

"Nice job with the chrome, man," Ronnie 1 says.

I hear the clunk of the nozzle shutting off and Kev 1 walks back around to top off the tank. Ronnie 1 looks at Kev and says, "Twenty-four even," and Kev hands him a Visa.

"Can I see that for a second?" I say.

Kev hands me the card and I look at it. The expiry date is 06/20. The name is MR RON J POTTER. I just shake my head and pass the card back to Ronnie 1 who goes into the shed. I follow.

There is a counter and a stereo on the shelf and chips and chocolate bars that melt in the heat. I remember that. And there is a cash register and I know where they hide the money in the cabin on the hill and I know that I will one day lock myself out of this shed in the middle of the day and that a guy named Teddy with a hunting knife will break into the shed for me.

Ronnie 1 swipes the card on the old imprint machine, pushing hard on the handle as he moves it from one side to the other and then back again to imprint the numbers. He checks the slip to make sure he can read the card information and puts it on the counter for me to sign, which I do. He takes the slips and separates the copies, giving me one and taking one for the till.

"Where are you guys from?" he asks me.

All of a sudden I am exhausted. I feel faint but I answer him. "Sunderland. I live in Sunderland and Kev lives in London."

"That's that guy's name too," Ronnie 1 says, nodding toward the pumps.

"Really," I say. "Are you guys from Whitney?"

"No," he answers. "I'm from Newcastle and Kev is from Oshawa. This is a summer job for both of us."

"Oh," I say. "How do you like it?"

"To be honest, I'm a bit homesick," Ronnie 1 says, looking out the window. "I miss my family and my friends. I never thought I would. Sometimes Kev and I close here at seven and drive all the way home. He drops me off in Newcastle and goes home to Oshawa and then picks me up at four-thirty so we can drive back up here again."

"That's a lot of driving in one night," I say.

"Six hours," he says. "We drive six hours to be at home for six hours. And we sleep for three of them. It's crazy."

"Not really," I say. "When you get to be my age, it makes good sense, really good sense. You can really get to missing people."

He looks at me. "How old can you be? You don't look old."

"How old do you think I am?" I ask him, thinking this is an opportunity to get some clue as to how I look to him.

"I don't know," Ronnie 1 says. "You could be forty or you could be sixty. You're a hard one to pin down. How old are you?"

And I realize that I know how old I am. "I'm fifty-four."

"What's it like to be fifty-four?" he asks, looking me in the eye. It's me asking me about my life.

"It's great, man. I have a wife and a daughter and a grandkid. I have a horse and a house and a pretty good job." And I look back into his eyes. "Life is what you make it."

"For sure," he answers and goes to walk out into the sunshine.

"This little room gets hot," he says.

I just follow after him, observing his strong muscular back and his tight ass. I admire his ass and his strong legs and his long silky sun-bleached hair.

That was me, I say to myself. That was me.

I FOLLOW MYSELF OUTSIDE. Kev is talking to himself from inside the truck. I walk around and get in the passenger side while Ronnie 1 stands in front of the ice cooler. I wave and he waves back. His straight-backed stance is cocky, proud, invincible. "Where did that kid go?" I say out loud. Kev just looks at me and starts the truck, pulls out and turns left back toward town.

"What were you guys talking about?" I ask him.

"Hockey, girls, Catholicism, the prospects of military college."

"Wow, you got pretty deep," I say, looking around my shoulder at Laddie in the back.

"I'm good at interviewing people without them knowing it. Remember, I was a pastor for a quarter of a century."

"Okay, Pastor," I say. "Where are we going now?"

"Well, Ronnie, I think that if we find a place where we would like to stay the door will be open and no one will be home. And I always loved that white house beside the rapids where we swam. No one was ever there and I always felt like it was a house in a dream."

"You would have liked to have stayed there instead of the cabin?" I am laughing. "The cabin, the goddamned cabin. With no soffits so the bugs came in as readily as kids to a party with free beer. Except it was free blood. Aranka hated me talking about the Stones and that cabin."

"Don't go there, Ronnie."

"Where, the cabin?"

"No, the old life. If I start thinking about Cathy and the boys I will be sucked right out of here into my old life."

"Oh, I get ya. I'll give you something to think about that will root you right back here." I start to guffaw. Kev looks at me with a grin and his head tilted.

"The shitter," I say. "Remember the shitter."

He exhales and leans his head against the driver-side door jam. "Whose idea was that thing?"

"It was mine. I remember going up to the cabin and you said there's no toilet. You were going to go and buy some Canadian Tire thing, like a camper toilet, and I could just imagine emptying liquid shit into the bush every morning."

"This is funny. This is funny," Kev says. We are going about ten miles an hour but no one is on the road, which is strange, but everything about this is strange so I go on with my story.

"So I found that oil drum. And I found some concrete blocks and I dragged them up onto that big flat rock, back in the bush so no one could see us. And I found some two by fours in the cottage and there was a hand saw and some nails and I made the wood seat and I sanded it down so there would be no ass splinters and I made two braces to go down into the drum so you wouldn't slide off and I put the drum on four bricks and I made three steps out of the bricks so you could step up and sit down to shit."

"It was like a real throne, Ronnie. You sat up four feet off the ground with your bare ass on a steel drum," Kev says, putting the top of his fist against his forehead. "I can't believe we lived like that for a whole summer."

"And remember your really straight friends came for a weekend and the tall guy with the big nose was sitting up there and you had me go into the bush and make bear sounds while you hid and took pictures."

"He would have jumped off and ran back to the cabin with his pants down if I hadn't called out to him," Kev says. "He was so mad, but he forgave me. Eventually he even came to appreciate the joke."

"Actually, I really liked that guy," I say. "I remember sitting at the fire with a beer and him telling us how someone dropped acid on him at a party and he didn't know what happened. He just started feeling weird and he left the party and sat in a park all night. He thought he was going insane." I look over at Kev. "He believed he was losing his mind. He said he couldn't think straight, he couldn't collect his thoughts. He said he was so sad, thinking he would never be normal again. It was like this clown I once saw in Cirque. He was standing in a torrent of paper scraps with a huge fan blowing like a blizzard and a huge light shining through and he was holding his hat and mourning his friend who had died. It was so sad. And your friend telling that story about sitting alone and losing his mind. He experienced an immense sadness. I remember asking him why he didn't go to the hospital, and he said, What's the point? He had lost his mind. And he sat there alone all night and in the morning he was tired and went home. What happened to him?"

"He was going to become a doctor but he started doing small theatre as a kick and eventually he started acting full time. The dark night of the soul, Ronnie." Kev winks at me. "We have all had them."

"At the time I thought your friend was so brave. But he didn't have any choice, really. He had to experience what life had handed him. But I admired how he handled it." I look up at Kev. "I once freaked out and locked myself in a room because I was too high. Another time I went home and asked my dad to sit up with me. But your friend didn't ask for help from anyone. He just toughed it out."

"I think it takes more courage to ask for help, Ronnie. It's harder, I think, to admit that you are weak and could break than to soldier on like you're invincible. Remember, I was in the military and that is what they taught us. I was tough. I knew self-reliance. But it failed. I became arrogant. I hurt people and thought I was doing the right thing. And anyway, there are always helps, invisible helps and helpers. Remember, I'm dead. I've been on the journey of the soul. I know things you don't. We are never alone. That night, Smoulders was not alone. That was his name, John Smoulders. There was an old man, a street person, three yards away on another bench keeping an eye on him. John never knew. The old man was sucking in all self-destructive thoughts. That old man was his saviour. That old man had once been John in that same park and had committed suicide. He had done it. And now he had returned to prevent it happening again. And it didn't."

"Like a pre-cog," I say.

"Like a what?" Kev shouts.

"A pre-cog, who knows the future and can prevent it. It's an old Philip K. Dick term."

"No, Ronnie. Not like a pre-cog, more like a guru who can suck up karma. The things that happen are formed by our thoughts and actions, from this life and past lives. We don't even understand what's happening to us. And there are gurus for all of us and they can absorb karma and prevent future events from happening. We all have them. They are our guardian angels. They are actually our future selves coming back in something like a circle."

"Like a pre-cog," I say. "Like Millson said."

"Who, what?" Kev shakes his head like he has water in an ear.

"My old friend Dale Millson always said life is a big spin. And he was right. What you are saying makes me think of a perpetual motion machine. It generates its own energy to continue generating its own energy. We keep cycling back and going ahead and back and ahead. It never ends."

"No one has ever seen the end anyway," Kev says. "No one wants it to end because when it ends it's over. We're over."

"We are all waiting, aren't we?"

Kev nods. "Yeah, Ronnie. But no one knows what for."

"It's insane," I say, but Kev leaves it at that.

We drive back into town and turn by the inn and drive up beside the river. The road ends but a single-lane grass road continues. We have driven here a hundred times before. Of course, like Kev has pointed out, we are making this up from our memories. So we have made up an empty house that is in our memories, a shared memory. We parked twenty yards from this house every day for a whole summer and never saw anyone here. So we can extrapolate from that memory. We can create from that memory but we cannot create ex nihilo which means from nothing. Only God can do that.

18

We pull up beside the house. It has a concrete step to an aluminum storm door that leads into a porch and a white solid wood door that leads into the house. There is a small picket fence around the front yard that is also small. Kev walks up and opens the screen door and enters the house. I watch from the yard. He comes out again.

"It's empty. No clothes, no food, nothing but furniture."

"I guess we won't be staying long anyway. Let's go get chicken and beer."

Kev walks back to the truck and I follow. He gets in the driver's side and I get in the passenger's. He backs into the grass driveway, long grass and daisies, and turns and drives back toward town. We cross the highway and turn into the Brewers Retail. I go in and pick up a two-four of Export Ale. Looking around I see familiar faces. I see Peter who has a house on the hill where huge parties are held. I went to a pig roast there when Kev was away one weekend. I know that Peter will commit suicide next year because his parents find drugs in the house and force him to move back to Toronto. I see the doctor, a middle-aged guy with a long beard, looking like the guy from Seals and Crofts. He screws every good-looking woman he diagnoses. I see Karen, with crazy red hair and tall like a model. I know she gets killed in a car accident next winter.

"Hi Potter," she says.

"Hi Karen," I answer. My face is burning hot.

"Going to Connie's party?"

"When?" I answer, pressing my forehead with my palm.

"Tonight. How could you not know? Aren't you dating Patsy?"

"Oh yeah," I say. "Well, it's complicated. Her old boyfriend's hanging around."

"That fucker," Karen says. Now it's her face turning red. "He cheated on Patsy. He screwed that cunt in Barry's Bay. Now he wants his sweet Patsy back."

Her pretty nostrils are flaring out of her pretty nose while she pushes her index finger into my face. I notice the manicured pink fingernail. I am staring cross-eyed at it when she forms a fist and punches me on the chest.

"He's a two-timer, Potter. Kick his ass. Just kick his ass."

I shake my head like I could wake up if I shook it hard enough. I look at Karen and her intense green eyes.

"I will kick his ass. I know I will. Consider it done."

She steps back like I just became a different person.

"You do that, Potter," she says and backs away and turns and walks out the door. I go to the counter, take out my wallet and see that it is stuffed with cash. I laugh because Kev and I always carried the cash from the till in our wallets. We figured it would never get stolen that way. I pay and carry the two-four out to the truck. I have forgotten Kev but he is right behind me.

"Did you hear that conversation?" I say.

"Thrilla in Manila. Or Thrilley in Whilley or the Catastraska on the Madawaska. Ronnie defends his girl. History in the making."

We start to laugh. "You know that we'll be spectators. I will be watching myself do something that I have always wondered about. What would have happened if I had just walked away?"

"Ah, but you are now the pre-cog Ronnie. All the karma that created that experience has been absorbed by you being here. This will be different. This will be very different."

I lift the case of beer into the back of the truck. A steel Coleman cooler is in the back. Laddie stares at me and does not move, even as I jump into the truck.

"Who are you, the goddamn Buddha?" I say.

"You wouldn't even have known who the Buddha was when we worked here."

"I know," I answer while carefully transferring the beers from the case to the cooler. "I didn't even know what a Jew was when I started working in Toronto. I thought it was a religion like a Catholic."

"And all black people were Africans?" Kev says, leaning on the truck bed.

"According to Peter Tosh all black people are Africans," I answer and stop. "Right now, Tosh and Marley are two young guys in Jamaica playing ska in garages, maybe doing some local gigs."

"Stephen King just published Carrie and Patty Hearst just robbed a bank," Kev says.

"And this is the first year the Flyers won the cup," I say and close the cooler and tuck the empty case behind it at the front of the truck box. "Let's get some ice."

We drive back to the gas station to buy ice from ourselves. As we get close, I see in the side mirror that Laddie is up with his face in the wind.

We turn in and Ronnie 1 gets up off a lawn chair. Led Zeppelin III is playing and the music is flowing out the open door of the shed. We pull up and stop and get out of the truck.

"Dazed and Confused," I say. "I haven't heard that in ages."

"You shoulda been here a few minutes ago," Ronnie 1 says. "The song just started and this chick comes in, cut-offs so short her ass is hanging out and a thin shirt, a guy's shirt held with one button. And she is so high, dancing and swaying. I go out to pump the gas but she stays in here and the other guys who are with her are just shaking their heads. They pay me and call her but she just keeps on dancing until they have to go get her."

"What did they call her?" I ask him. My palms are sweaty and I have that sandy feeling in my gut. I look at Kev.

"I always told her I had met her here. I described it to her just like this."

"You know this chick?" Ronnie 1 says.

"No," I say to Kev who is about to speak. "Hang on." And I turn to Ronnie 1 and ask, "What did they call her?"

"It was a weird name, like Anka or Arka."

"Was it Aranka?" I ask him and turn to Kev with my index finger in the air.

"It was, it was. How did you know, man? You must know her," Ronnie 1 says, looking at me with some sort of recognition.

"Chances are," Kev says, "you are going to meet that girl again one day."

"I don't know, man. Girls like that are pretty fucked up. They'll mess your head up," Ronnie 1 says. "I would get so possessive of a girl like her. If someone messed with her, I'd end up killing them. And someone is always messing with girls like that." He looks at me. "She's way older than me anyways."

"Yeah, ten years to be exact."

He looks at me with furrowed forehead.

"How do you know that, man? You must know this chick. Or you're from the future or something."

I half turn to look at Kev and then I look back at Ronnie 1. "Can we get a couple of bags of ice?"

"Sure, man." He opens the ice freezer, reaches in and passes me two bags of ice. Kev is already up in the truck box and I pass the bags to him. While he is dumping them in the cooler over the beer, I pay Ronnie 1.

"Big party tonight," he says. "You guys should come."

"Oh yeah? Where's it at?" I answer and again turn to look at Kev.

"Why do ya keep looking at him like that?" Ronnie 1 asks.

"Oh, to see if he wants to go to the party."

Ronnie 1 shakes his head and passes me change. "It's at the house just up by the cop shop. There'll be tons of people there. Not just young people. There'll be older folks like you guys too. You should come."

"What do people do at these parties?" I ask him.

"Get fucking pissed," he answers.

Both Kev and I laugh.

"Sounds like fun," I say. "We'll be there."

Kev jumps down from the tailgate and I get in the passenger side. Ronnie 1 goes into the shed and Kev gets in the truck, starts it up and pulls out and onto the highway.

"I thought you were going to blow it," he says.

"How can you fucking blow it? If I told him the truth, that I am some future version of him come back to fulfill some sort of karmic function and he doesn't recognize me because his fucking consciousness would explode across the fucking universe, he wouldn't believe me. He would think I was completely off-my-stick insane." And I pause.

"Kev. Can you imagine what Aranka looked like? Can you imagine her here? I told her once that I met her at the gas station."

"And what did she say when you told her that?"

"She blushed, she fucking blushed because it was her."

"How many years were you married?" he asks, again leaning his head on the doorframe.

"Fifty-three years, man," I say. "We were good together."

Kev smiles and nods but I know he is thinking of his own marriage and his own three sons.

"You died too young, Kevvy," I say. He looks at me and his eyes have become distanced.

He doesn't answer. And I leave it at that.

19

I look back to the road, to the double dividing line that curves with the asphalt, at the emptiness of forest and evergreens inhabiting their own shade. "Let's go get chicken," I say.

"Good idea," Kev responds. "It will be nice seeing the place again."

We drive through town. People wave. I assume by the familiarity of the gestures that we are in our younger form once more.

We pull into Arnold's, a chicken palace pool hall converted from an old gas station. Our old comrade David, one of the local Whitney boys, is sitting on a bench outside having a smoke.

"Boys," he says in greeting, lifting a Coke can in salute.

"David," I answer. "What's up?"

"Nuthin'," he answers and takes a drag on his cigarette. I notice it is so short he seems to be burning the filter. I follow Kev who has already gone inside. Chub shouts "hey!" and laughs with his cherub Indian face.

He is standing at a pool table, cue in hand. Goose is bending to take a shot. Goose is ten but talks and acts like a sixteen-year-old. And a sixteen-year-old in Whitney is like a twenty-year-old anywhere else. His long blond hair drapes over the table as he stoops to aim. I wait and watch while Kev goes over to Albert to order the chicken, Albert with his crew-cut shaved military head and his oversized body.

"Ronnie, half chicken?" Kev calls. I just nod and continue to watch Goose.

"Fuck," he says, still leaning on the table and bowing his head to the slate.

"Goose," I say.

He looks up. "You big fooking Moose," he says. He is the only person up here who caught on to my nickname from Newcastle. "Buy me chicken?"

"Okay," I say and call to Arnold standing behind the chicken counter in his grease-stained white apron, crew-cut hair and black-rimmed glasses. He looks like a giant-sized Drew Carey even though Whose Line won't be on TV for another two decades. "Arnold, two more, one for Goose and one for Chub." Chub is smiling Cheshire-like and nodding.

"Thank you, thank you," he says in mock Chinese.

I am thinking two decades in the future when Chub is going to call me from downtown Toronto. He will tell me he is stranded and needs a car repaired to get home to Whitney. I have not spoken to him since now and at the time of the call I am well into my thirties.

"Give the repairman the phone and I will give him my Visa," I say to Chub after saying how happy I am to hear from him.

"No, no," he says, "the guy only takes cash. Can you send it by taxi?"

"No, Chub," I answer. "I know what's up. I've been played like this before. I'm a Christian now and I don't do this shit. I'm clean, man."

"Oh yeah. I'm a Christian too," he says and then says so long and hangs up. I don't know if Kev knows this story so I walk up to him now, in the present day, and say, "Your brother Bob came up to me at your funeral." Kev looks at me out of the side of his head. "He stayed in touch with Whitney. He found out that Chub comes back and becomes the Indian chief. He does all right. He was pretty fucked up for a while, living on the streets and doing hard shit."

"How do you know that?" Kev asks.

"He called me once begging money. But like I said, he comes back and becomes chief."

Kev nods and smiles. I can see him settling into himself. I guess he's like me. Living these memories brings real emotions. Mostly of fondness. As I stand here with these guys I look at them all as God must look at us. I love them. Everyone an individual. Everyone on the stage for the first time in history. Everyone playing his part for the last time in history. I put my arm around my cousin, squeeze his shoulder, watch him smile again.

"Here you go, guys," Arnold calls and we all go up and get our dinner and sit down at a table. I pick up my chicken, greasy and spicy, take a bite and wash it down with a Coke.

"Hey, Potter," Chub says. I look at him as he talks between mouthfuls. "Gueva's coming to the party."

"He's a beggar for punishment."

"He's pretty tough, you know," Chub continues.

"What are you, Chub? His fuckin' coach? Are you in his corner?" Goose laughs, throwing his head back. We all laugh at Goose.

"I just want Potter to know in case he doesn't want to go," Chub says, still smiling with his round cheeks.

"I can handle myself," I say. "If he wants Patsy and she wants him, he can have her. But if he wants a piece of me, he'll get it."

"Ooooh, Potter," Goose says. "He'll take a cheap shot if he can get one. That's his only chance. If he faces you straight on, he'll get a hidin' laid on him like he never."

"I kinda feel sorry for him. He seems lonely. Does he have any friends?"

"I don't think he has any friends other than Patsy," Chub says. "At least I never met any of them."

We all go quiet and focus on our chicken and potato wedges.

"I'm goin' for a swim," I say, getting up with my tray. I walk over and put it down on the counter for dirty dishes. The plate is china. The utensils are steel. The only garbage is the Coke can. We are just beginning the McDonald's era, I think to myself. The era of unlimited garbage and unlimited soda. I hold the plate for a moment. The weight, the colour. I can feel the colour. I look up and Arnold is watching.

"Nice plates," I say.

"Thanks for putting them up. It makes life a little easier."

"You're welcome," I answer. "Now for that swim." I look at Kev and he just waves me on.

"I'll catch up with you later," I say. And I exit the chicken place into the bright sun and the heat, take a moment and bask before I start to walk up the river road.

20

I walk up beside the green painted concrete brick building, up past the small inn with the gardens and the black and orange granite rock that the river grows around, up the road with the wildflowers: daisies and cornflowers and purpled blue-bell blossoms. A gull circles overhead, with double-V wings and tips of grey.

The water churns down the rapids with a roar like heavy static blaring. I walk up to the white house and then down a path opposite to a rock outcropping. I stand ten feet above the water and strip off my clothes. The water is deep and dark and seemingly bottomless, even though I know you can touch bottom if you jump hard enough. Curious ripples circle on the surface, clues to the strength of the current. I dive in and the cold swipes my back and I am rushed downstream to the chute where the water spills over a ledge and onto a jutting boulder. I put my legs forward and am pushed in a torrent of silver spray until my feet brace me and the water hammers me—neck, shoulders, back. My legs push and I am one with stone,

one with water, one with the elements of my birth here, on this planet, in this solar system, in this galaxy. I let go with my feet and spill into the pool below, slow water with slippery rocks and weeds that grow randomly, sprouting out of the water in long green blades. I walk to the edge, climb over the sharp stones to jump in and do it again. And as I emerge onto the path I see Patsy walking up the lane. She is squinting in the sun and has on her normal white T-shirt, shorts and sandals. She hurries as she walks, a little short walk with light steps, almost a shuffle. A short girl with large breasts and a muscular body. But she's as careful as a Catholic. I think she let her ex fuck her and that is why she hates him so much. I think she hates herself for letting him and she hates him for not being what she thought he should be. She does not see me but my clothes are beyond me so I walk out into the open.

I see her cover her nose and mouth with both hands and stoop and screech with laughter.

She runs up to me and I stand waiting. "Potter, skinny-dipping in the middle of the day? Really?"

"You should try it," I say.

"Not here. I wouldn't jump in there if you paid me."

"I will," I say.

"What?"

"Pay you," I answer.

She pushes me and I step back, laughing.

"I ain't no whore, I'll have you know."

"I know that," I say, stepping forward to embrace her. She pushes me away, full force with both arms.

"Put your fucking clothes on. I can't have you standing here naked. It's too weird. Now put them on."

"They're not here. They're up there." I am having fun being an unrecognized middle-aged person disguised as a teenager. Nakedness is not a problem in your fifties.

"Then go get them," she hollers and points to where I methodically wander.

"Wanna beer?" I ask after I return clothed, then, "Shit." I realize Kev has the beer but no sooner have I said it than I see the green Ford's front end coming up the lane.

"Wanna beer?" I ask again.

"No," she says. "And anyways, I just wanted to say hi and make sure you were coming tonight."

"I'll be there," I say. "But I hear your ex will be there."

"You don't worry about him," she says. "I told him to stay away, but if he comes I'll take care of him. And I don't want you to talk about him. I'll see you later."

"No need to get pissed," I say.

Kev pulls up, hangs his head out. "Hey, Patsy. Where you going?"

"I have to go get ready for the party. I'll see ya later."

"Want a ride?"

"Sure," she answers and walks around to get in the passenger side. Kev smiles and waves and backs the truck out the lane. I watch the two faces recede with the windshield, down the lane and around the corner. I watch the back of the truck move off into the distance until it is gone.

And I feel confused. I feel as if I have been played, like I am a pawn in this story. I felt that so often around girls. And I am feeling it now.

I go back and sit on the concrete step. The flies buzz in the heat. They land on my arms and knees. What is the point, I am thinking. What is the point of being here? Already nothing is the same and the unfamiliarity of the situation is unnerving. I feel jittery and anxious, feelings I have always known. Soon the fire is before me and I am my old-man self once again.

This is what death feels like. It's scary as hell. Birth was even scarier but we never remember it. I don't know if it's possible to recapitulate the birth experience. From warmth and comfort and safety into light and air and noise. It must seem like a lifetime inside that womb. And I am sure we experience all the emotions of our mother's outward life. But I also think that we are more of our spirit selves then, more aware of everything that makes spacetime exist. So maybe, possibly, we are strengths for our mothers. Maybe we share consciousness. And I once read that mothers are more in touch with spirit because of giving birth. Because the pain of the experience forces them out of their body. Or maybe it forces the connection with spirit. Women are different, for sure. Maybe that is why men have always thought we had to protect women. Because they are so vulnerable during pregnancy and birth and then with the infant. And they are so different. They are more organic, more resourceful and intelligent. Men think they're the stronger and smarter, but if there was a war between men and women, women would survive. Men would obliterate the world, but women would survive.

Goddamn it, even the Bible says the woman is the weaker vessel, but that idea all went to shit during my lifetime. I had a dream once. There was a castle with a large courtyard with a stone cobblestone floor and large stone-block walls that rose a hundred feet on all four sides.

It was big enough to hold thousands of people and there were thousands in there. It was some sort of celebration and everyone was cavorting and mingling when this giant dragon came and started to kill people left, right and centre. And I jumped into action because somehow it was up to me to save everyone, especially my darling wife who just happened to be in this dream with me.

So I ran to where this dragon was and jumped up to slay him but he kicked my ass and I was lying in my own blood and broken teeth. And this woman comes in leather and light armour like some hot Viking goddess and jumps on the dragon and sticks her blade in him over and over. He tosses her around and she gets cut up and broken pretty good but she kills him and saves everyone. Then she comes to me and says, "You couldn't have done it. Only a woman can slay the dragon."

What the fuck? Whitney has changed. Patsy was not like that. Kev was not like that. Or was I remembering everything wrong? And this is my whole point. We have no objective reference. We only have our memories, which are only thoughts after all. And as easily as I can imagine some hot thirty-year-old standing naked in this forest with me, needing my fire and my warm body, I can imagine my past and call it a memory. And that leaves me bewildered.

21

"Hot thirty-year-old?" Kev says. He stands beside the creek, Whitney age.

"Shall we?" I say. "Invent some? Hot thirty-year-olds, I mean."

Kev laughs. I notice the change in light. Morning is coming and the birds are singing from inside the bush. It feels like summer. There is dew on the ground instead of frost.

"It was cold when we left here to go there," I say.

"How do you know?" he answers and laughs, still looking at me.

"I don't know," I say, looking at and stirring the fire with a stick. "I should know but I don't."

"We have to go back," he says. "We have to go to that party."

"Why? I don't like it. I don't like what's happening there. My life is being changed before my eyes. I don't like the feeling of not knowing what's going to happen," I say.

"I don't think you have any choice, Ronnie. The unknown is calling you. Your time on this side is up."

"And what if I don't go?" I say, standing up. "What if I just say no to the goddamn unknown?"

Kev is smiling as I approach him. His eyes are like mirrors that reflect my image back to me. I am my Whitney self.

"You can't," Kev says. "You can't say no to the unknown. Your path is plotted, Ronnie."

And the next thing I know Kev and I are pulling up in the old green Ford pickup, up to the brown wood bungalow under the pines by the cop shop.

"Fuck," I say as Kev parks on the gravel opposite Patsy's house. We get out and I jump up in the back and pull the cooler to the tailgate. We each take a handle and lift it off.

"It's heavy," I say.

"We're not as young as we once were," Kev says with a huff and a chuckle.

"Depends on who's watching who," I say and we both laugh so hard we must set down the cooler. We can see the fire in the yard beside the house throwing reflections over the lawn. Skids are stacked to the left and the hardwood is popping and sparking like fireworks. And the people are just shadow spectres walking around while wood smoke carries the voices to us. I open the cooler and pass a beer to Kev and take one for myself. I always had an opener in my pocket when I was here, so I check my jeans and sure enough a chrome-plated plastic-handled Molson Canadian opener emerges with a hexagonal hole in the top. I crack mine and pass it to Kev and he passes his to me, which I crack for myself.

"We're down there, you know."

"I know, Ronnie," Kev says. "Are you nervous?"

"Nervous as hell," I answer. "I've never seen myself like this. The other times, like when I punched the ref, there were adults around and the police came. But this will be raw."

"Yeah, it's lawless," Kev says.

"I'm lawless," I say. "Or I will be when Gueva gets here."

"Look," I say. "There's Bung and Choog." Bung is Choog's older brother and reputedly the toughest character in the area. Bung sees me pointing and comes over and shakes my hand. He looks like Burt Lancaster with an old lumberjack shirt rolled up at the sleeves.

"Hey, Bung," I say. "Have a beer." I open the cooler and lift out a dripping brown stubby, pop the cap and hand it to him.

"They say there'll be a fight," Bung says to me.

"Really?" I answer, looking at Kev and lifting my eyebrows.

"Uh-huh. The girl's being harassed by her old man. Her new boyfriend, the kid, says he will lay a hidin' on him if he comes around."

"Is he here?" I ask Bung. "The new boyfriend I mean."

"Yup, over there." Bung points while I look. I look and then look at Kev. Kev is looking too.

"There we are," I say, sidling up to him so Bung can't hear. We are standing on the opposite side of the fire, talking to the sisters, Patsy and Bonnie. Kev can't help stooping and laughing out loud.

Choog comes over. He looks like a curly-haired Paul Newman. I remember a really hot blond girl came to town from Chicago to stay with her grandparents. She was tall and slim and sixteen. Everyone wanted her, even the older guys, but she went for Choog. Choog with his leather jacket in the summer and his pointed shoes and his chains.

Choog doesn't recognize us any more than Bung did.

"Bung," he says, "who the fuck are these clowns?" He takes three steps away and turns and takes three steps toward us. He has a cigarette between his index and middle finger and he points it at me, shaking his hand, making charcoal flares in the dark.

"I know you, but from where?"

"There he is," Bung says, interrupting Choog's thoughts. We all look to the fire. Gueva has come. He is speaking to Patsy's brother who walks over to Patsy and talks to her and then leads her over to Gueva.

"He's sucking up," Choog says, walking toward us. "He's saying sorry for screwing that Skinner chick. He says he didn't do it, but she says he did. Patsy believes her." Choog laughs, spits and coughs. Bung laughs too because he overheard Choog's explanation to us.

I look at Kev and he laughs too. It's all so absurd.

I notice out of my peripheral vision that Choog is looking at me.

"Who'd you say these guys are, Bung?"

"They're just some guys visiting town," Bung answers. "They say they know us. They say they know Annie and Albert and Raymond."

I look at Kev, who shrugs. "Did you say that?" I ask him.

Moose

"You should get lost, boys," Choog says, staring off toward the fire and pulling a drag on his smoke. "We don't like strangers in this town. Something might happen."

"I'm not leaving," I say, almost absentmindedly. "I've gotta stay and see this."

"See what? A fight?" Choog answers, turning to face me. I turn and step toward him with my shoulders braced.

"Listen," I say, "you have me confused with someone else. I am not a friend." But I'm stopped in my words by Bung, who steps between us. As I speak over Bung's shoulder I am overcome with emotion. I see Choog's face and it glows. His face just glows and I smile and say, "Listen, you young fuck."

Choog steps back and laughs.

"You remind me of someone," he says, his voice drained of intimidation. I reach in the cooler for another beer, pop the cap and hand it to Choog.

"Cheers," I say smiling, lifting the beer.

"That smile," he says. "Bung, I know that fucking smile."

"You're crazy," Bung answers and turns his attention to the small group that has gathered around Patsy and Gueva. I have been watching all along. Patsy has been standing with one brother talking to Gueva. Now her other two brothers are walking up to them and they form a huddle that makes it difficult for us to see.

"There's a lot of tension in that huddle," I say. "Something's about to happen." And then Gueva steps back stooping and holding his nose and then stands, holds out his palms like he's pleading. Patsy steps out from the group, short Pumpkin Patsy, and she is yelling at him and gesturing, but we can't hear it. Gueva stoops and turns and walks away.

"I think she hit him," Bung says.

"He keeps holding his nose," Choog adds, laughing.

"Dumb fuck," Choog says.

"Patsy sure can pack one," Bung says.

We watch as Gueva turns back and holds up a palm in surrender and begins searching the ground. Then he is on all fours, crawling around. Patsy's brothers push everyone out of the circle. Soon they are on the ground searching too. And then Patsy has joined them.

"They're looking for his glasses, Bung. Patsy knocked them off him when she hit him," Choog says.

Patsy stands up holding them and stands before Gueva and puts them on his face. Then she reaches up and pulls his shoulders down to hug him.

"See that?" Choog says. "It's just like a woman. You let 'em punch you in the head every once in a while, you can pretty well do what you want."

I look over at Kev.

"Kinda anticlimactic? Wouldn't you say?"

"Yes, Ronnie. That describes it perfectly."

"Let's go down to the kitchen and I'll describe what happened. Or what didn't happen."

As we are going down, I see Ronnie 1 talking to Gueva.

"You know, Kev. After the fight I never wanted to be with Patsy. I could see she still wanted that Gueva. In this reality I must have realized that before I punched him out. Saved myself the trouble."

"You saved yourself something, Ronnie."

22

We step up onto the porch and enter the house. It's one of those sixties' places with the old chrome and Arborite table and plastic padded chairs with veneer panelling on the walls. We go into the living room and it is dark with just a corner lamp turned on. I point to the couch, a long brown corduroy davenport with wear patterns and large flat pillows.

"She was here." I point to the couch. I see Choog has come in with us but I don't care. "She was lying on that couch with Gueva behind her hugging her to him and they were asleep."

Choog steps up, laughing. "And you said get up, you fuck. Get outside because you were going to kick his ass for being dishonourable or some shit like that. I remember thinking, What the fuck is Potter talking about."

"And then what happened, Choog?" I am smirking at Kev, thinking that things have become bizarre.

"He got up to follow you and you were here." He steps into the doorway between the kitchen and the living room. "And Gueva jumped you from behind and you ran forward and then back like this into the fridge." Choog runs forward and then back into the fridge as if he were me. "And then you smashed him into the wall over here." He backward runs into the east wall between the counter and a set of cupboards. "And you split the panelling here and then you turned and jumped and landed on your back right there." He indicates the floor. "You had hold of Gueva's legs like he was a kid getting a piggyback and you jumped and pulled his legs at the same time so he landed right under you and he smashed his head hard and let go. And then you stood up and kicked him. You were wearing work boots and you kicked him in the side and in the head. He was hurting, you could tell. And then you said—" Choog starts laughing. He holds his gut he laughs so hard. "You said, How does it feel to be slagged by a fourteen-year-old? Patsy was standing there and she said, Well, that explains a lot."

I look at Choog and he continues to laugh. Tears are in his eyes when he looks at me. I am not laughing as I look back at him. He sobers up pretty quick and says, "How the fuck did you get here? You're the adult Potter. You shouldn't be here."

"Is it real, Choog, or is it a dream? Everyone here believes this story. But there is another story and you and I know it. No one else does."

"Ah, but Potter, I died young. Crashed my Yamaha. So now I am dead and alive at the same time. I see things and then I forget them. Like I see you and I will forget you. But for you to be here like this, kinda like me, you musta died young. There's no other way."

"No, Choogie. I started this journey as an old man. I was married to a fantastic woman for a long, long time. I didn't die young."

"Yes, you did. You surely fucking did."

I go outside. I need to get away from Choog. Kevin seems to know something but he isn't telling. The summer night is cool and I am cold. I wish I had a jacket. The fire is sparking and flaring, making its own commotion. I walk over and stand in its radiance, absorbing the reflections of flame into my skin.

"Where's your beer?" I hear Chub's voice say. Goose is with him. They are treating me as my young self, oblivious to what just transpired, acting normal toward me. As if normal is a term to be employed.

"I don't know. But I sure fucking need a cold one right now."

"It's up on the hill there, Potter. Oh, it was, but now it's here and there's some missing. Hope you don't mind?" Chub says. Goose guzzles a beer beside me.

"Ah," he says, lifting an empty bottle to the night.

"You drinking our beer?" I say, looking at Goose.

"Yup," he says and lets out a long intense burp.

"Well, help yourself and grab me one when you're getting yours," I say. And in a moment a cold Molson Export appears in my hand. I watch my former girlfriend in the arms of her boyfriend and I remember the relief at being rid of her. The relief of not wanting to be wanted.

Kev and Choog come down out of the house. Choog is the Choog I've always known, but Kev is young again. Ronnie 1 and Kev 1 have gone. And I figure we have become them in another fucked-up consciousness transition.

"Goose!" I yell.

"I'm right here beside ya."

"Get Kev and Choog a beer."

"Coming right up," he says and darts off into the dark.

"Chub and Goose have hidden our beer," I say to Kev. He smiles knowingly. The fire is raging in hot flames that are invisible at their base.

"See that flame?" I say to Kev.

"Uh-huh," he answers.

"It's a magic flame," I say. "Know what it burns?"

"No," Kev answers. "What does it burn?"

"It burns karma, Kev. It turns our past to dust."

"Profound," Kev says. "Profound shit."

"Goose!" I shout.

"I'm right here beside ya, Potter."

I look down to my left and the little Goose is watching the fire.

"Three more," I say, tipping the stubby in his direction. "Or just bring my cooler."

"I'll bring the cooler," he says. "Better than bein' your slave." And he vanishes into the dark to re-emerge moments later with Chub, each toting a side of our Coleman cooler. They set it behind us on the lawn.

"Thanks, Goose," I say and reach for another beer. I pass one to Kev and one to Choog, one to Chub and Goose. We all brandish openers except for Kev. I open his. And I raise my bottle to the night.

"Here's to the fire that burns karma," I say.

Choog and Kev laugh but Goose looks at Chub and says, "What the fuck?" But we all drink.

"I'm exhausted," I say to Kev.

"I know you are," he answers.

"I'm going," I say and leave quietly like I'm off for a piss. I turn to look back and Kev is watching me. I enter the bush and look back. Kev is still watching.

I step and stumble in the dark. The sound of voices and the cracking of the fire fade as I reach through cedars and plod through mud. I scratch my face on a low branch. I stoop almost to my knees and block branches with my bare arms. I can see the road as I push farther and then I emerge in the grass ditch which I cross onto the gravel shoulder and the smooth black pavement with the yellow lines. I walk west.

23

My shoes grip asphalt, my lungs fill with damp air, my nose is distinguishing pine, mud, weeds, smoke from the fire. My arms and face feel the cool night's breeze. I remember walking this road and always being afraid a bear might appear. I am the same me but I have no fear. Instead I feel my body's weight on my feet and how my balance shifts to accomplish movement.

It is about two miles to the gas station. I am no longer exhausted. In fact, I feel like I could walk all night. There are no cars on the road. It's not like when I started this story, in the third millennium, forty years from now. Then, there will be so many fucking cars. Everywhere cars. So many people as well. Unimaginable to me now, here in Whitney. The sky is a barrage of stars. Like when I was a kid, I would press my eyelids against my eyes until these spinning L's would appear, spinning like wild little black boomerangs. And the backdrop was white, white-white. Like an infinite liquid with no inconsistencies. With these spinning black L's. And then they would fade and sparkling dots would appear, every colour and they were not reflecting light. The light came from the place. It was in everything, sparking colour with so many points that you could not begin to contemplate counting them. That's what these stars over me are like now. The beauty is everything. Everything is beauty. I believe I am in an egoless state right now. That's why all this is apparent to me. I know this because of knowledge I will acquire in the future. Sounds funny, doesn't it. Because of what is happening to me now, I doubt that I will be myself in the end. That old man with the cancer may become a dream or a myth.

I start to laugh and I start to skip. I remember skipping as a small boy. I loved it. It was one of the first things I learned to do. I am skipping on the highway. And I remember that horses skip. It's called a canter. I remember sitting on a horse and doing this and then switching. It's called switching leads and so I switch my feet to having the left forward and then I switch again and have the right forward. I stop to walk and catch my breath. I ride a horse in the future, I say to myself. I remember that too. I laugh. I am remembering backwards, I say to myself. And I continue to walk to the cabin.

I make it to the gas station.

Moths and giant insects are forming a moving halo around the lights over the pumps. The gravel driveway up to the cabin is dark and I walk up to find Laddie sitting at the door, whining a greeting. I open the door and we both enter. Turning on the light I observe the room, a memory come to life. There are two beds on each side covered with clothes and sleeping bags in disarray. I stoop and untie and step out of my boots. Work socks, I am wearing work socks. It's the middle of the summer and I am wearing Grebs and work socks. There is a kitchen table in the middle of the room. Kev has some textbooks and spiral notebooks piled up. I remember he had some school stuff he was working on during the summer. He became an engineer, I remember that. He even went to Oxford. Not that this young brat I am now would even know or care what Oxford represents. But to me as I am, with all my knowledge of the future, I realize it is quite an accomplishment.

This room is like a time capsule. I am here with my cousin's things. When he died he was a pastor who helped other pastors with their problems. He tried to resolve divisions between church leaders and was successful in many cases. He had his God experience when he was young. He left the army where he had become an officer and trained with the Salvation Army instead. He had three sons and was kind of a Fred MacMurray, an all-around nice guy. After this summer in Whitney we drifted apart. We both got married young. He moved to London. I moved to Claremont. Forty years later he was overweight and went on some herbal diet pill and that's what killed him. He had friends who were doctors. He was in some goddamned place like Japan when he took sick and he stayed in the hospital, in intensive care for months until he became stable enough to send home. And then he was in the London Health Sciences for months. The doctors loved him and tried everything. The best in the country were looking after him. I think it was his pancreas. The new diet pill blew out his pancreas.

His funeral was hours long. My mom, my sister and her husband, my wife and I all went. It was boring as hell, but still, all these guys went up and told everyone how Kev had helped them.

I see his school stuff piled up on the table. I look through and take one of the spiral notebooks and a pencil from the table and go to the bed, prop a pillow against the wall and sit back to write. I will write a lot in my life. It will become as fluent as hockey is to this fourteen-year-old boy-man. Laddie jumps on the opposite bed, curls up and looks at me for a moment before he curls his face into his body. Dogs, I think. All our lives surrounded by dogs. I settle back and breathe, invoke the spirits and relax. The events of this evening have released something and with it gone I find a peace, even a sense of humour about life. Even thinking about Kev and his life has produced a calm. Because he is here now and this is reality. This non-reality is reality and it shows me that reality is a non-reality. Basically, that nothing is real. Like the Bhagavad Gita and Krishna and Arjuna, where it's not real and detachment from actions and results is the order of the day. And because of that you go for it. You give it hell. Fight the war, Arjuna, because you need to. Because it is your destiny to kill or be killed. But it really doesn't matter. Because you and your enemies are all one in the end, part of the great self, the great oneness.

And that's like me and Kev. We came here and it became different than it was four decades previous. But only we know it is different. Choog knew, but that was because he died. I haven't died yet and I wonder when I will.

24

When I started this journey I was fifty-four and trying some of the new-age stuff, some of the shaman stuff. Then the old geezer took over and I was him, alone and dying. And now I'm me, here in Whitney. And now I'm different. I have detached from my life. Like a rocket ship detaches from the engines and floats in space as a capsule. That's what I am now, floating around my life, able to look at events the way Apollo astronauts could look at continents.

I remember my journey to Whitney started with recapitulating my relationships with women. That got me here. I wanted to recapitulate the energies still in my body, energies that would keep me in places where weariness infused everything. I wanted to be done with those tired roots of my existence. I wanted to be free to explore, but like a space shuttle I needed to get beyond gravity.

They made a movie in the future called The 40-Year-Old Virgin. I must laugh. I was the nineteen-year-old virgin and even that seemed a very long time. There were close calls before that. I'm going to tell the story of one of them. Or I'm going to write it. I am going to sit here propped in this bed in the cabin and write in this notepad. No moving around for a while.

I had this aunt, Aunt Jean. She was a speed freak at one time. Stories populate my past of her stoned out of her mind. Once with all her friends in my grandparents' basement, all of them lying around stoned and naked and how my overly Catholic grandmother walked in on them. Apparently, they didn't even notice her. But at the time of this story she had quit the heavy dope and was just a drinker and a pill popper. I remember her giving me valium for a bush party. I rode my bike like it was an antigravity bike, or like it was made of rubber.

But Aunt Jean, even though she had quit dope, married a guy who did a lot of dope, my Uncle Greg. And they moved to Newcastle. There were five houses on Mill Street just south of the four corners. Jean and Greg were in the middle. It was a party zone. It was normal small-town life in the seventies. Everyone partied.

Two houses down from Greg and Jean lived Debbie and her kid. Debbie's husband was a biker but they had already split up. I knew this because he had paid my uncle a visit when I was there. Greg was sitting on the porch. He had a porch on the front of his house that looked out onto the street. I was riding my bike past and saw him up there and stopped and walked up.

"Hi Ronnie," he said. He was six-four with a wild afro and a body like one of those Hawaiian guys, soft and smooth and kinda fatty. He looked like he was part African with big lips and a flat nose. And when he talked he kinda sputtered his words. I went up on the porch to sit with him.

"What are you doing?" he asked me.

"Just riding around," I said.

"Got any dope?"

"No," I answered.

"Too bad," he answered with a huff like a cough.

"What's the axe for?" I asked him.

"Protection," he answered.

We sat there for a while, not talking. He was sipping a Blue and the Eagles' Hotel California was playing in the background. And these guys came walking up in biker leathers. They had crests but I wasn't paying attention. Because I was nervous. They were walking without talking. I saw Greg's left hand grip the axe.

There were four guys. One guy with dark hair, long bangs and a big moustache that covered his mouth and dark whiskers like he hadn't shaved for days. He was short and the other guys were taller but skinny like him. They had long hair but I pretty much ignored them because he spoke.

"Stay away from my wife," he said. He had a gruff scratchy voice like the singer from Steppenwolf.

"Or what, Frank?" Uncle Greg said, lifting the axe by the handle so the head was before us, like it was the message.

"Or we come up there," the guy answered.

"Well," Uncle Greg answered, "I plan on seeing Debbie as often as I want. And I invite you to come on up. But one of you will go back down, hard and fast. I don't care what happens to me, but one of you is going to fall." Uncle Greg gently lowered the axe. "Who will it be boys? Who will it be?"

It was funny to watch Greg get aggressive because he had a tiny scratchy voice that betrayed his massive body. And he was always sweating. Like now he had on shorts and no shirt and bare feet. He had hardly any body hair and a soft belly and a dimple of a crevice between his breast bones. But he was fucking scary and those guys just turned and walked back down the street.

It didn't take long for Debbie to destroy Greg's hope. She became friends with my Aunt Jean and confided to her about Greg's visits and come-ons. My aunt was tougher than those bikers and Greg stopped going to see Debbie.

But word came out that Debbie liked me. She'd seen me at my aunt's and I certainly had noticed her. It was summer and she wore a halter top with some frills at the edges and flowers embroidered across the front. It was more knit than material and if you looked really close you could see the darker nipple underneath. Her shorts were really short, cut-off blue jeans with frayed edges that exposed her hips and the top of her legs. She wore flip-flops on her feet and her toenails were painted pink and perfect. She had a thin face with red hair that hung in ringlets and a cute nose that looked like it had been broken once. And lips and teeth that were small like her cheeks and jaw. Her legs were long, frog-leg long, and she was fit, her belly and her thighs ripped with muscle tone. She was twenty-eight and perfect. I was sixteen and a jerk. My body had grown too fast and I was always crashing into and breaking things. I didn't talk much because I was so self-conscious. The only times I was confident was in some sort of conflict. Then I would emerge with confidence and eloquence. Maybe that was why I was always immersed in conflicts and turmoil. Some hormone would kick in and I would be Super Moose, ready to avenge.

The day I saw her at my aunt's, I was riding my friend's 350 Honda Enduro motorcycle, a road-dirt hybrid. All my friends had bought Yamaha 650 roadsters and they were going for a tour and one of them suggested I take the dirt bike and go with them. After about thirty miles my hands and arms were numb from the vibration so I went home while they went on cruising. I went to my aunt's and Debbie was here.

"Hi Ronnie," she said. "I'm having some people over tonight. You could come by if you wanted."

"Sure," I said. I looked at my Aunt Jean, dark black hair and black opal eyes, looking as Irish as a bottle of Guinness. She was always trying to get me laid. She had another beautiful friend of hers over one night and I was there. "The plan was in the works," she told me later. "We were going to get you on the couch." But then the girl's husband paid an unexpected visit and those plans were shot. But I could see she wanted Debbie to have me.

I went to Debbie's house that night. She had a fire in the backyard and it was all young people there. Most young people in Newcastle were broke. I had a job and could buy booze and dope. I drove up with the racket of the motorcycle drawing everyone's attention. I got off, took off my helmet and walked up to the crowd.

Debbie stood, crossed her arms and then her eyebrows when she saw me.

"Whose is that?" she said.

"It's my friend's," I answered. She had on jeans now which slung around her hips like a loose-fitting harness.

"I thought you had a car."

"I drive my dad's," I answered. "He's giving it to me soon."

She shook her head and looked at the fire and took a drag on her cigarette. "Well, I'm glad you made it. Do you have any money?"

"Yup," I answered.

"Enough for a bottle of whisky?"

"For sure," I answered.

"Let's drive to Oshawa and get some booze."

"Okay," I answered, thinking some whisky would go down nicely. I was nervous and totally out of my league. But when I got nervous I said very little which people perceived as nonchalance. And I had this big-guy stance, hands in pockets, shoulders back, watching everything. That unnerved people. I was doing it now. I could see Debbie getting nervous. She was probably thinking I would leave. She was right. It was too awkward. I was going to leave.

A girl by the fire was holding Debbie's kid. Debbie tossed her cigarette in the fire and said to the girl, "Keep an eye on him for me." The girl nodded her reply and bounced the kid on her knee a couple of times. The girl was blond and the kid was blond and anyone would have thought the kid belonged to the girl.

Debbie went in the house and came out in a jean jacket and tossed me the keys to her 1967 wine-red Pontiac Bonneville convertible. I had passed it in the driveway.

It was a nice car but had seen better days. We walked to the car and I got in. The doors were heavy and wide and swung hard. It had black bucket seats with cushions to sit on because the leather upholstery was torn and a shifter on the console between the seats. The ashtray was overflowing with butts and the back was full of bags of clothes. It was a nice night and the top was already down.

I started the car and at it rocked from side to side, like it was running on four cylinders, which it probably was. I backed out of the drive with her in the seat beside me and dropped the shifter into drive and clacked, clacked, clacked away. There was a hole in the exhaust manifold.

"Your car needs some work," I said to her.

"But she runs," she responded and put her hand on mine which was resting on the shifter. We drove up Mill Street and turned left at the lights. I was taking Highway 2 to Oshawa, to the only liquor store I knew that was open after six p.m. We talked a bit.

"What do you do?" she asked me.

"I work midnights at the Esso on the 401," I answered.

"Doing what?" she asked.

"Pumping gas and diesel," I answered. "Ever heard that Frank Zappa song?"

"Who's that?" she said.

"He's a musician. Have you never heard him?"

She just shook her head and looked straight forward.

"Who do you listen to?" I asked her.

The car is a convertible and this is my first time driving one. The wind is cool and nice. Her hair is blowing off her face. I am looking at her. She is beautiful, model beautiful.

The steering wheel is huge and the car steers like a boat. It sways like a current is pushing it.

"Who's that?" she asks again. "That Zappo or something."

I feel like Johnny Depp playing Hunter Thompson in Fear and Loathing. I am losing touch. Is it possible that I am in this car with the hottest woman I have ever known? I was just in Whitney in the cabin writing on a notepad. But now I am here.

"Frank Zappa," I say. "Wind Up Workin' in a Gas Station is one of his songs. My friend Mike and I just went and saw him at the Gardens."

"How was it?" she asks.

I stop my adrenalin to answer her. "It was like being at something that you only get to be at once in a lifetime," I say. "He had this band, there must have been ten guys. Synthesizers, xylophones, bongos and all kinds of percussion and bass and guitar and a huge drum kit that was high up overlooking everything. And Frank sitting on a chair smoking cigarettes, getting up every once in a while to sing or play lead guitar. Two guys beside us offered to shoot us up with speed for free."

"Did you?" she asks, sitting forward and looking at me. I smile. I am much older now than the kid who was sitting beside her a moment ago.

"No," I answer her. "We were way too young to be hitting speed."

"But you're still that young," she says.

"Yes," I answer, "still too young. Who do you like?" I ask this fully knowing the answer because I have done this once already.

"Burton Cummings," she says. "I love Burton Cummings."

"His idol was Jim Morrison of the Doors," I say.

"Oh," she says but I know she barely has a clue who Jim Morrison is. I wanted to suggest to her that it was impossible for Burton Cummings to idolize Jim Morrison and still turn out the fucking gay shit he wrote. But I thought better.

We cross into Oshawa and turn down Simcoe Street toward the liquor store.

"Stop here," she says, sitting forward and pointing.

"For sure," I say and look for parking and pull in.

She turns to me wide-eyed and smiles. "Let's go in for a drink."

There is an old hole in the wall bar on the corner. Kind of like the Queens in Newcastle, really old, red brick with a painted sign that says CADILLAC.

I may be sixteen, I may be fifty-four or I may be eighty. But there really is very little difference. I remember all of this happening but now I am here while it is happening. And Debbie gets out and I get out. She walks up and puts her arm around my waist, turns and grabs me by my shirt and pushes me against the car, pressing her body hard against mine. She kisses me. Her crotch is on my crotch, her tongue is in my mouth and I taste menthol tobacco and I am responding as best as I can. I think to myself, I am an amateur with a professional. Like playing chess with a Russian or being in net and letting Bobby Hull take a slapshot. But then I think, no, I have had sex hundreds of times and I lean into her with all the verve of my being.

She releases me, steps back and smiles. "Wow, Ronnie. That was something."

"Yeah," I say breathlessly.

But I know how this plays out. We go back to her house and the pizza delivery guy comes and doesn't leave. I know him, Terry Thompson, a buck-toothed fuckhead, but she must have screwed him because he has the idea they are a unit and are heading for Vancouver as soon as he saves enough money by delivering pizzas. But I play along. What guy wouldn't? Patsy and Whitney played out differently. Maybe this will too. I decide to ask her as we are walking up the street.

"Hey, Deb. Do you know Terry Thompson?"

"The pizza guy?" she answers.

"Yeah, that's him."

"Yes. He's weird. He's always coming on to me. Why do you ask?"

"Because I had this dream." She stops walking and faces me. Her smile is lopsided as if amused.

"You were dreaming about me?" She pushes into my belly and chest with her front.

"Oh yeah," I answer. "More than once. But this dream was different."

She pushes off me and we stand apart.

"In this dream we are doing exactly what we are doing now. And then we go back to your house and you pay the babysitter and put the baby to bed and then you put on Burton Cummings and we slow dance in the living room. And then Thompson comes and knocks and you let him in. He freaks when he sees me there. And he asks what am I doing there like I'm the intruder. And then he tells me a story that he is taking you and the baby to Vancouver to live with him. You tell him he should go but he won't. I tell him to leave or I will kick his ass but you say to leave him alone and I do. And you and I go into the bedroom but nothing happens. You even leave the door open because you don't trust him. And we lie on that bed all night while Thompson plays Burton fucking Cummings all night. And he dances like he's running on the spot, thump, thump, thump, thump. That's all I remember. Thump, thump, thump, and the stupid Cummings' voice screaming. We never became intimate and he never left. Just Burton fucking Cummings all night."

I look at Deb. She looks at me. I expect a reaction. I put a lot of emotion into the story, not on purpose but I got caught up. She touches my hand.

"Ronnie," she says, "that guy has never been past my front door."

She takes my other hand and pulls my arms around behind her back. "You have a weird imagination," she says and lifts her nose to kiss me, to which I respond naturally.

We go into the bar which is long and mirrored on one side. Guys and ladies are sitting at the bar and at the tables and they all turn as Debbie struts up in front of me. Her hips are alive and every part of her that counts has a movement or a quiver as she walks.

Oh my god, I think. I must look like a goof with her. She stops and I pull out a chair and she sits. "Thanks, Ronnie," she says with a smile and a tongue pressing her cheek. I can see that she knows what she's doing, and she loves doing it.

"What will you have?" I ask her.

"A Blue."

"Two Blue," I say to the bartender, who is only across the aisle from us. He nods and returns with two cold beers dripping condensation. The place is hot and Deb takes off her jean jacket. Her shoulders are muscular and so are her arms. She smiles to me because I am so closely observing her.

"Do you work out?" I ask her.

"Just a bit. I hate pigeon shoulders." She takes the beer and sips while looking around. I overhear some guy say something about me being a punk. He says it loud enough for me and everyone to hear.

"Losers," Debbie says. "Ignore them." And then she says, "Do people talk about me?"

"Yup," I answer.

"What do they say?"

"Rumours and lies," I answer. "Rumours and lies."

She lifts her beer to her lips again and drinks while looking sideways at me.

"You're mature for your age. I watch you. You don't act your age."

"That's because I don't know my age." I cough and sputter and hold my nose to prevent the spurting of beer. Debbie laughs and holds her nose for the same reason.

"You know what," she says. "I believe you."

Silence settles between us. I want to tell her about how I came back here, into this time and this body. I think she's on the cusp of being able to understand. I am looking at her and she is looking away.

25

"Greg doesn't touch me," Debbie says.

"He loves you," I say. "He talks crazy about you."

"I know," she answers. "I adore him like a brother but not the other way. Even though he protects me."

"From your husband?" I suggest.

"My ex-husband," she answers, tilting her beer for another drink. "He gets rough. I told Greg. Greg told him that if he did it again he would get rough with him. Have you ever seen a man hit a woman?" She looks directly at me.

"Yes," I answer, looking away.

"Did your dad hit your mom?" Her voice is soft when she asks.

"No. Dad would never hit Mom. It is his cardinal rule. A man should never hit a woman. He says that if a man hits a woman he is a cowardly piece of shit, or something to that effect."

Her eyebrows cross. "Who then? Or do you not want to talk about it."

Moose

I sigh and exhale. "Okay, I'll tell you. My cousin and I were working in this small town up north and Greg's parents had a cottage about an hour away. Greg and Aunt Jean were there and they invited us to come up and go water skiing. So we did. We were going to stay over and leave early in the morning to open the gas station. We went skiing and had some beers and a barbeque and then Kev and I crashed in this bedroom with bunk beds. It was funny, sleeping on bunk beds, but it was an old cottage with four rooms. And they got in an argument. And Jean just started putting Greg down. Saying things like he was no good, that he was a disappointment to his parents, a lousy husband and father. She just went on and on, bringing up the past, old fights they had had. Greg started yelling at her to shut up. Just shut up Jean, he said, but she just went on and on. It was like she was trying to humiliate him. I don't know why she didn't shut up. She was drunk and drunks are stupid like that. And then slap and thud. From the sounds we knew he had hit her and she had hit the floor. But it didn't sound like a punch. It sounded open-palmed like a slap. Kev and I got up and walked out to leave. Aunt Jean was sitting at the table crying and Greg was standing. He apologized. Sorry boys, he said. We just said our goodbyes and left. I remember Kev saying how weird it was. We were both really quiet on the way back to the gas station. We never understood it."

Debbie put her hands flat on the table and looked at her rings. Her mouth withdrew into a thin line and she exhaled and dropped her shoulders. I thought of Shakespeare's Ophelia and Judy Garland and how innocence and beauty create such vulnerability. I realized I had always loved Debbie and that was why I had returned.

"Did that happen to you?" I ask her.

"Not the same," she answers me. "I never asked for it." She lifts the beer and guzzles it. I follow her lead and do the same.

"I don't think Aunt Jean was asking for it either," I say. "She was asking for something but not that." I look at her. "What do you think she wanted from Greg?"

"I don't like this, Ronnie. I don't like this conversation."

"Want another beer?" I ask her. She nods. I signal the bar for another round.

"I was on the porch when your husband came to see Greg."

"Frank has avoided coming around since then."

"I guess Frank is your ex?" I suggest.

"Yes," she answers. "He was a nice guy. He was shy but a lot of fun. He was good to me. But bikers think different, and when he joined them he changed."

I can see a change in her. Like something rising up. She sits taller and shakes the hair off her face and shoulders.

"They pass you around. They think you should be available. It's like some old tribe of warriors and sharing your woman is an honour. I couldn't take it. I wouldn't do it. I can't tell you more. I just can't." Tears are now forming rivulets on her cheeks, but she doesn't wipe them off. She reaches for her beer and shakes her head again to loosen the hair that has fallen on her forehead. She blows at a tuft and smiles at me.

"This is pretty heavy stuff for a kid."

Moose

"Sometimes I feel like I've lived three lifetimes already," I say and laugh.

"Maybe you have," she says, observing me. "You are very old in your ways."

"Oh shit!" she says and sits up in her chair looking toward the door.

I turn around and see a guy who has just come in. He's tall, my size with a white T-shirt under a leather vest. He's short-haired, moustached with a day's growth of beard. He has chains for his wallet and rings and tattoos up his arms.

"Deb," he says. And then he looks at me. "Who's the kid?"

"C'mon Ronnie," she says and grabs her purse and hurries past the guy. I stand up and go to follow but he blocks my way. I go to step around him and he moves. So I just stand face to face with him.

"Punk," he says, "stay away from her or else."

I see two guys in similar attire come in behind him. They form a triple-post effect, like a door in a horse paddock. I look at my adversary and say, "We're just friends, friend." He still doesn't move until the bartender calls out.

"Don't make trouble, Bill. Or leave now before you get started." And then, "Let the kid leave."

Bill looks over and nods and steps aside. I walk past him and between the other two and through the door. I can see the back of Debbie's head in the car. I walk over and get in the driver's side. I sit and fumble for the keys. I am keyed, that is what I think.

"Jesus Christ, Ronnie," she says. "That scared me."

"It's okay," I answer. "No harm done. But I am way out of my league with those guys."

"There's always a group of them, Ronnie. You never see any of them alone. They're a gang. They're bullies. They always outnumber their victims. I detest them."

We both sit in silence. I insert the key in the ignition, start the car and drive away slowly.

I look at Deb but she is looking straight ahead.

"Why, Ronnie?" she says. "Why so many assholes in my life?" I remain quiet. I know she is going to talk.

I pull into the liquor store. "I'll be right back," I say and get out and go inside. I take a card and write the number and go up to the counter and hand it over. I pay and in a few moments a guy comes back with a bottle of whisky in a bag.

"Thanks," I say and go back to the car. I pass the booze to Deb who immediately unscrews the cap and hauls a long gulp. She passes it to me and I take a long guzzle for myself, cap it and put it on the floor.

"Do you think I'm beautiful?"

She takes the bottle in the paper bag again and unscrews the cap and lifts the bottle to swallow. She passes it to me and I take a second swallow and replace the cap and put the bottle on the floor. I start the car and look to pull out. I look at her face. Tears are a film on her cheeks.

"Beauty is trouble. I've had more terrible experiences because of my looks than you can imagine. Are you going to be a terrible experience, Ronnie? I don't want it. I don't want you to become a terrible experience. But somehow, something feels wrong."

I drop the car into drive and get out onto Simcoe heading south.

The night is humid. Her legs are crossed in front of her. I look and shake my head, thinking that she will ask me to leave because of my age, because of my inexperience. Because of the trouble that I could become.

"Don't worry, Ronnie," she says as if reading my thoughts. "Tonight I'm all yours."

26

I turn onto the ramp and onto the 401 and head east. The wind is cool on my body. The humidity is a fog that obscures everything on either side of the highway until we reach the Ceresdale Fertilizer silo with its brightly lit lettering. I get off on the Mill Street ramp and head north past my own house, past the church where Dusty's funeral was held and into the driveway of the white bungalow with the blue door, eaves and shutters. She gets out and walks before me, up the concrete steps to the concrete porch and into the house. I follow her inside. The babysitter gets up off the couch.

"Ronnie, do you have a ten?" Debbie asks. I separate a bill from a crumpled wad in my pocket and pass it to Deb who passes it to the sitter.

"How was he?" Deb asks her.

"An angel. He fell asleep right away."

"Thank you, Kim," Debbie says and holds the door for her to leave. I am watching out the front window. I am trying to sort my thoughts but they evade my grasp. I only know what I don't know. I don't know what I'm doing here. I don't know what's about to happen. If I am about to get laid it is not going to be frivolous sex. Maybe I should escape, because the emotional intensity I am experiencing is overwhelming. This woman is a tragedy and I am about to join her. And I will join her. This has become destiny, to be here with her in this house on this night. I am all in. I am going all the way.

"Hang on," she says after closing the door behind the babysitter and disappearing down the hall. I move to the sofa and sit down. I see the stereo lid open and I go and look. Burton Cummings is on the turntable. Break It to Them Gently is one of the songs. I remember the lyric about a guy on the run. Am I on the run?

I remember when this happened the first time. I went home and the old man was so pissed. He was sitting at the kitchen table smoking. Mom was up and about. I could tell she was nervous. She was trying to do dishes without much success. It was more like moving things around. "Where were you last night?" Dad asked me. We weren't on good terms. His hands were locked above his elbows that rested on the table. I was once afraid of him but I wasn't anymore.

"At Debbie's," I answered.

"Goddamn it," he said and smashed the table with his fist, bouncing the ashtray. "A goddamn tramp, that's all she is. And my son being at that house."

I could see Mom starting to cry. She had her back turned to us. She had on a blue housecoat over pajamas. I turned back to him.

"She's not a tramp. You don't know her. And if you have anything else to say let's take it outside." I had squared off with him before. He was a tough guy. His arms and chest were muscled. He was old school. At this point in my life I didn't like him very much. He thought he knew too much and he didn't like to listen.

Now I am thinking I would have liked to tell him the story. About how hot Deb was and how I was certain I was going to get fucked and how Terry Thompson came and ruined my chances. It is a funny story. We could have shared it. We could have laughed. "Listen Dad," I would have said, "this is what guys do. They try to get laid. You would have done the same thing in my shoes." And then I would have lightly punched his shoulder and said, "C'mon. You probably did. C'mon, tell me the story of how you lost your virginity." That's what fathers and sons should do, dialogue the experience, discuss how sex drive overcomes the best morals. And then talk about what fun it was to do it, to finally fucking do it.

But all he ever said was "never use a woman." And he also said "you can never understand a woman." And he also said "don't get married too soon, maybe not at all." And these are the thoughts running through my head when Debbie re-enters the room.

She stands in the door. "Ronnie, close the curtains," she says and I do. My palms are sweating and I feel sand in my veins. My heart is a jackhammer in my chest, pounding with a rhythm I have never felt before. She steps forward. Small breasts, teardrop-shaped, and the faint outline of ribs and the belly and bellybutton and the soft expanse of hip and thigh with the red tuft of pubic hair, small and wavy like the hair on a little kid that Mommy is always trying to comb into place. And bikini areas, untanned and white skinned, making her look more naked than she already is.

"I'm so nervous," I say.

"Don't worry, Ronnie. I'll teach you. I'll coach you." She smiles with the tongue pressing the cheek again. And then she licks her teeth. She comes to me, takes my hands and guides my arms around her and presses against me. I kiss her and she kisses me in return. I step back, pull off my shoes, my T-shirt and jeans and underwear and stand naked with my erection in front of her, feeling like a hairy ape-man in front of Raquel Welch.

We made love, sitting on the rug with my back against the couch and her on my lap. We did a lot before this. For instance, she gave me fellatio and taught me what muscles to contract so I could control ejaculation. She would hold me in her mouth and just as I was about to explode she would poke me with a fingernail just behind my scrotum and I would stop and she would continue.

She taught me cunnilingus and showed me with her fingers where to move my tongue and how to stimulate her with my mouth. She taught me how to finger her and how to bring her to orgasm by massaging her clitoris. She taught me that over and over. In fact, she may have become overstimulated because she kept saying no more, no more.

But when she sat on me and guided my erection into her, we became cosmic. Seriously, I couldn't feel my legs and there were bright coloured spots in front of my eyes. When I released into her I released everything, every emotion evaporated like the rain-soaked earth in the hot August sun, steaming and moistening the air, filling the atmosphere with humidity. All my joy, pain, despair, hope, ecstasy dissolving through this union. This was the dissolution of the ego.

As I relax her into my embrace I say, "We are timeless."

And she answers, "I know, Ronnie. I know."

She begins to weep, with her head on my chest. Sobs, and she reaches her arms around my neck and I feel her relax, and like a baby settles into a deep rest, so does she. I sit like this for a while. Her breath becomes slow and deep and I reach under her and adjust her into my arms. Pressing off the couch, I stand and carry her to the bedroom and place her on the bed. She is light. She curls into herself. The bed is unmade so I can just pull the duvet up to cover her. I am not tired and I remember the whisky in the car. I get dressed and decide to go out and get it. I peek out the door before I go to make certain Uncle Greg is not on his porch, but the coast is clear. I rush out, reach in and get the bottle and rush back. Because after all, I am trespassing. I am trespassing on my uncle's, my dad's and possibly my own morals. I am trespassing into a situation that can never turn out right. I am the ogre taking the maiden. I am the Phantom. I have used the ability to transverse time to come here and use Debbie. That's what I think. That I have no right to be here. That this is all wrong. It's the old Catholic stuff. You know, I will be punished for this and all that.

27

I TAKE THE WHISKY INTO THE BACKYARD AND SIT AT A PICNIC TABLE. The smell of the spent fire is like sweet burning charcoal. There are some plastic cups on the ground and I take one and pour it a third full from the bottle. The taste is sweet and harsh, hot in the throat and mouth. I look over at the neighbours' and see a baseball bat. It's one of those aluminum ones. You can't break those. That might come in handy, I say to myself and cross the small wire fence to get it.

And I remember from the future. Chekhov's saying if a gun appears in a story it will have to go off. I am thinking of Bill and the bar and how he will tell Debbie's husband and how we may get a visit tonight. I am like that. I think ahead. I have always been a thinker.

I should be tired. I have no idea how late it is. This is real. This is what I am thinking. I keep saying it over and over. I am being redundant, deliberately, like I might convince myself. This has never happened before. I sit on this bench sipping whisky and listening to the night. Cats screech and yowl in a garden next door.

How late is it? How long were Deb and I at it? I laugh out loud, but not too loud because Deb's bedroom window is open just twenty feet away. I realize everybody's windows are open, because there are no air conditioners. In my day the droning of compressors is non-stop in the hot weather. It is a soft knowledge that tells me this world is so much simpler than the one I left. The night is cricket sounds and a baby crying and a man coughing. Most of these doors are not even locked. We never locked ours. I could walk home right now and go up to my room and turn on the fan and sweat the night out.

It's hot. Even now in the nighttime.

It's funny how I called the future "my day." This is my day. I am here. And I notice everything. A bird calling syllabic notes with variations on a theme. He sings the same song but changes the octave, just enough to make it different while remaining the same. Deb has a flower garden along her fence. Like really, a chick like her has a garden. If you saw her car you could not imagine her in a garden, but it is beautiful. There are irises and hostas and roses. In the future I will help my wife with her garden quite a bit. And I will come to like it. But now it smells like an exotic liquor, sweet and perfumed with a sour touch, like gin or something. And again I laugh. It's sweet but a little bit stinky, like sex.

Sex is amazing, I am thinking. Naked bodies become something else. Deb and I made love for a very long time and our bodies were who we were, not some glamorized presentation. We spend so much time thinking about how we look, but once you are naked and with someone you just are. I read a lot of consciousness stuff before I got here.

Actually, that is how I got here. But sex with Deb was just that, the expression of pure consciousness. My wife and I would have sex like that sometimes. It's funny. You lose yourself and become entirely one with consciousness. It's scary. Old ego has a hard time with this kind of stuff.

In the future I will read Seth, an entity who speaks through a medium named Jane Roberts. Seth knew Jane and her husband Rob in previous incarnations. He is a metaphysical teacher who teaches that only the present actually exists. Both past and future are constantly being altered through our choices in the present. Much of what got me started on this journey began through the teachings of Seth. And those books are being written right now in the seventies. Jane died young so the books stopped. And just think, right now I could drive to Attica, New York, find their house and tell them all about what I have done. I could talk to Seth through Jane. I wouldn't want to tell her that she dies in a few years. That is the downside of knowing the future. But then again, Seth said the future is based on possibilities and that there are many futures that are possible. Yes, of course. That is what I have been doing, exploring possible realities. I wonder if I could drive to Utica and sit in on one of Jane's ESP classes?

Who knows? If I stay here I could stay with Deb and help her raise her kid. I could figure shit out. Although everything could change. Maybe everything has changed. I refill the cup and take another sip of booze. I am a little drunk. Like I said, maybe everything has changed. Maybe Seth never happens. But he must happen, because many things have not changed. The cast of characters is consistent with my memory. But what if memory comes with the place? Seth says that there is only one moment ever happening, and that we create our past the same way we create our futures, by projecting from our now. It's like this: you want to experience something so you create a past to justify its existence. Nothing is real. But does that mean that we are puppets of a big mind that stands behind us sending us here and there like actors in a movie and that we have no choice but to live out the script? That's what C.S. Lewis thought when his beloved Joy died. He thought he was a rat in a lab experiment. And then he had an experience he couldn't quite explain. He only wrote one book after that. It's called Until We Have Faces. And then a little while later he died. And then, that weird fact that J.F. Kennedy, C.S. Lewis and Aldous Huxley all died on November 22, 1963? That always blew my mind. Were they one entity in three personalities? Seth said that Christ and St. Paul were one entity. With what's happening with me, it kind of makes sense. If you stretch this story out, I have become more than a few personalities.

I sip more whisky. And maybe I will just blend into the matrix of this now moment. I don't think so. Being the old man, the time in Whitney, Kev, and before that with my wife and daughter and grandson. No way. The funny thing, the thing that mystifies, is that from here, sitting at this picnic table, they are all dreams. All dreams that go off in different directions. What did St. Peter say in his epistle? "Awake, O sleeper." Wow.

I hear motorcycles on Beaver Street, one street back from me. They drive slowly, the engines barely a rumble. They are Harleys. The exhaust comes out in small pops like shotguns being fired into the earth. They stop. It is quiet.

And they're here. And possibly, I don't want to run to conclusions, but it is quite possible that they're coming to teach Deb a lesson. And if they think I have stayed around, they probably have planned something pretty for me as well. I reach down and grip the bat. And I remember a book by C.S. Lewis called Perelandra where a guy named Ransom gets taken to Venus where a new race of humans is beginning. And there is an Eve and a rival scientist who gets possessed by an evil spirit. Ransom ends up calling the possessed scientist the UnMan because his personality is remarkably void of any human empathy. Ransom found that the influence of the UnMan on Eve was far too powerful and the only intent was malice and harm. And after much soul deliberation Ransom realized he must kill the UnMan and he did, he brutally murdered the bedevilled scientist for the sake of Eve.

And here I am thinking this, like a stranger to this reality, holding a bat while men come toward this house, at least I think they are coming. I haven't seen them yet. Men who will exact vengeance on a woman with a child for not playing their game. She is Eve and I am Ransom and they have become the UnMen. And if they come, I will stop them.

I hear them. There are two fences for them to cross before they get to me.

"Fuck," I hear one of them grunt. "Fucking barbed wire. Who uses barbed wire for a garden fence?"

I laugh in spite of myself. I grip the bat and crawl beside the low hedge that runs along the back edge of

Deb's neighbour's yard. I hear the rustling of brush. They're quiet. I wonder what they are thinking. Are they nervous like I am? My teeth are chattering and I shake like I'm cold but I'm not. I imagine they are confident. They've probably done this before. Uncle Greg is confident as hell. He's kind of my hero, which might not be a good thing because Uncle Greg eventually dies in a knife fight. I didn't go to his funeral. I should have but I didn't. I distanced myself from the family after I got married. I had adopted a kid with more than a few problems and had enough to deal with without being concerned about my fucked-up relatives. But here I am with my future before me and I wish I had gone to his funeral. I wish I had said goodbye to him. I feel badly about it.

They are close. Who knows what is about to happen? Am I going to die? I have some weird premonition. Have I done this before? It's like a déjà vu. I grip the bat. You would think I would be filled with rage, seething with hatred. But I'm not. It's taking every bit of courage for me to stay here and not run away. I really am a coward at heart. I hate confrontation. In my life I was always known as a guy with a temper, a guy you didn't fuck with. If people really knew that my rage was a relinquishing of fear in a torrent of emotion, they might have laughed. And I had been taught anger by my old man. He was the exalted one, the general of anger un-management. So it was only natural that I released everything through aggression. Some guys would release it through tears. It's funny. I was always drawn to effeminate guys and women who could release emotion through tears. I would have liked to have been able to do that.

I think a lot of guys in the wars felt like I feel now, scared shitless in the face of the enemy. Was it because of duty? They stood and fired and got fired upon because of duty. I think so. I am standing here because of duty. Because someone has to stop these guys. And that someone is me. I feel wet on my fist which is pressing into the soil—a slug? A cute slimy slug. And now they are four feet away. I grip the bat with both hands.

I stand and there are three of them and the first one I see is Bill from the bar. His eyes widen and his mouth opens just before I hit him. The soft aluminum ting reminds me of kids playing softball. Bill falls to the left. I step toward Frank, Deb's ex, and swing the bat up and into his jaw. Blood spurts out his nose and his eyes roll back and he falls. I step forward and get him good again in the side of the head, thinking if anyone needs to die it's him. But the third guy runs at me before I get to raise the bat. He puts his left hand down on the bat and with his right he drives a knife into my side. I can tell it's a knife the way it enters and touches my spine, like a tickle, but I know I'm fucked. I cannot lift the bat and I feel the knife withdrawn and driven in again. This time it stays inside me. I feel no pain, just fatigue. I fall and I hear the guy running away.

It's funny, death is. It's like those old video games where you finally get shot up enough that the screen fills with red, like a stain spreading until it fills everything. My vision is like that now. It's filling with red and the world is leaving. I can still hear noises. The neighbour guy who was coughing is yelling. "Jesus Christ, Kay, call 911."

I hear Deb's voice. "What's wrong, Jim? What's happening?"

I turn my head. I can see her. I can see everything. I feel fine. I seem to be standing. Deb is a faint outline in the window. Is she naked? No, she has on some sort of pullover. And I see the neighbour standing over the bodies in a muscle shirt and jeans. I can see his bare feet and his big gut exposed like a hairy flop of flesh. I laugh.

"That's Jim. The plumber next door," a voice says from beside me.

I turn and look. Deb's husband Frank is standing beside me. And there's Bill standing beside him. They look exactly the same with biker vests and dirty hair.

"How the hell?" I say. "You're lying there dead with your vests and you're standing here alive with your vests."

Frank shrugs. "You're as dead as we are."

Bill says, "Everything here is a projection. It comes from somewhere other than here. Like in a theatre except the projector is behind the screen."

Frank nods and turns. He is watching people coming out of their houses to look at us. "That sounds reasonable to me," he says.

I see Uncle Greg come up the driveway and Debbie has come out with her long sweater wrapped around her. "What's happening?" I hear her ask Greg. "I'm scared," she says as he wraps her in his arms but he is looking toward us, toward us standing and us lying. He only sees us lying. Even I, newly dead, realize that we are invisible.

Then sirens and lights flashing, colours on the tall maples on the other side of the house.

Moose

"Wait here," I hear Greg say and he places Debbie by the shoulders into the arms of Aunt Jean who has just arrived. She is looking toward us as if she knows.

"I think Ronnie's dead," I hear Aunt Jean whisper to Debbie. She holds her head up, sniffing almost as if she were smelling, but I know it's an emotional thing.

"How did I hear that?" I ask Bill. "It was just a whisper and we're fifty feet away."

"The dead hear everything," Bill says. I look at him while furrowing my forehead and squinting.

"What? Have you been dead before?"

"Yup."

"But how?" I ask him.

"We're like actors," Frank stoops to say. "We turn up in other people's dreams and play roles."

"Whose dream is this?" I ask him. I feel anger. Frank laughs. "I guess it's yours because you're standing here dead with us. It usually ends that way."

Greg has come up to where we are. "Greg!" I holler.

"He can't see or hear you," Bill says. "You're dead."

Greg goes past us and looks at our bodies. He stoops with his hands on his knees and then grabs his thick Sly and the Family Stone hair with both fists and screams, "Ronnie!" with all of his voice. And then sobs, massive bear sobs.

I turn and see the police coming up the drive. One of them is my hockey coach, Joe Garney. Greg goes up to him like he's pleading. "It's Ronnie, Joe," he says. Greg is shaking all over like he's coming down. He's naked from the waist up in bare feet and jeans. The other cops pass. I see the ambulance guys rushing up with cases and stuff.

Garney says to one of them, "Look after this guy. He's in shock." And then he puts his hand on Greg's shoulder. "Sorry, Greg," he says.

"No Joe, no," Greg answers. "I need to be here when his dad gets here."

"Go take a stiff drink and get some clothes and come back then. And bring a drink for me too, Greg. Bring a bottle."

28

I notice that Jeannie and Debbie are gone. The ambulance guy puts a blanket on Uncle Greg and leads him away. Joe walks up to us and the bodies. I move close and look into his face. His face is a construction, held together by cop training. But I can see an energy field around his body, pulsing bright and then low, bright and then low. But then I notice everything is becoming colour. There's a lot of orange and red around everyone but the people are pulsing green. Some are blue. I can barely make out humans anymore because of all the colour. I make out the firemen when they march up the drive. They are all volunteer guys. My dad is the assistant chief. I know he will be here. No one could have told him. In the year 2015 they would have let someone know not to bring him. They would have the communications to do that. But not in 1976. I am fading. It feels like when I died moments ago. Weakness is all I feel. I am dissolving. I try to pull myself together. I feel hands on my shoulders.

"This always happens," Frank says. "We'll help you for as long as we can."

I come back together just in time to see Dad stoop over my body. The other firemen are helping him to stand up. He's like a drunk. Two men are holding him. One man goes to get a lawn chair. They sit Dad down and remove their helmets. That's all I get to see because the colours take over again, unimaginable colours.

It feels like I am swimming. It feels like I know where I need to go, like a salmon heading upstream to spawn or maybe like an exploding sun particle on its way back to a black hole. What was there doesn't exist anymore but even a vacuum leads somewhere. Maybe I am entering another universe. Maybe I am entering nothing at all.

Do not go gently into that good night,
Old age should burn and rage at close of day;
Rage, rage against the dying of the light.

Why am I remembering an old Dylan Thomas poem I learned in high school? Am I gaining consciousness or am I gaining awareness? Are we always conscious only without awareness? It's a good question. There are many blanks. Many things I do not understand. I know I am dead. This could be the reason for my silent rendering of Thomas's words.

Wild men who caught and sang the sun in flight,
And learn, too late, they grieved it on its way,
Do not go gentle into that good night.

I may be remembering this for a reason. Maybe I'm dead. Maybe I'm not. Maybe someone is telling me something. Maybe I'm all alone. Maybe it's me telling me

I have met my demise, capsized the craft, swallowed the pill, jumped off the cliff, so to speak.

I remember so many things all at once. Memories coming faster and faster, all faces, places, moments and it's all blah, blah, blah, all the same. The only thing I miss is the ability to care about them. But one memory stops the slideshow.

There is a little church on a dirt road. I remember the guys had converted a small horse barn into a meeting hall and then added a meeting room, making the barn an event room with a kitchen. It's summer and there are massive tree trunks with leaf canopies over the yard. There are kids running, chasing a soccer ball in a big open field between us and a house.

Ex-druggy, converted-Christian me is there in grey dress slacks and a blue short-sleeved collared shirt. I am skinny. For one of the brief periods of my life I am not overweight. My friend Don stands with me, dressed just about the same. We could be two Mormons but instead we are born-again Christians. Close enough. Don has been appointed as a kind of sponsor. He has been asked to disciple me, to teach me how to be a Christian, to teach me the faith. And it's good, it's all right because Don's from Oshawa and works in the Motors. He's a lot like me. We have shared a world of drugs and recklessness. Now we share a world of getting our shit together and trying to make sense of things.

Don has a beard and the composure of a Buddhist monk. He barely changes facial expressions and never changes his posture, hands in the pockets, leaning back, looking out at the world like he's seen it all.

"If you could ask God to do one thing for you, what would it be?" Don asks me.

I look around and up and across the road at the fields with young corn.

"God needs to help me to feel?" Don laughs. His eyes are blue and they look at me for more explanation.

"What do you mean by feel?" he asks me.

"I don't care. I really don't give a shit," I say to him.

"But you look like you care," he says.

"It's a ruse. I'm like a robot. I do what's right because I have a program running in my head. It's from my old man. And for some reason I want to fulfill it. I want to be a good person. But I am a blank, emotionally."

And then I look at Don. "Do you feel?"

He shrugs. "I think I do. I feel love for my wife. I feel joy, anger, despair."

"You don't show it much," I say to him.

"Pardon me?" He steps back and away from the conversation. But I keep on talking.

"I used to feel things deeply. But I couldn't handle it. I made myself emotionally numb like the guy in the Floyd song. Because the feelings were too much, too conflicting. Love and hate, guilt, remorse, self-loathing. That's why all the drugs and booze. I couldn't handle the emotions of my life, so I killed them. I drowned them in booze and neutralized them with dope and I felt better."

Don steps back toward me. "So why are you here, at this church?"

"Because I'm too young to die and I think that there may be another way to live. Maybe God can fix me."

Don looks at the ground, like what I am saying is making some sense to him.

"I think God can fix you," he says, still looking at his toes.

That picture fades and another one slides into view. I am standing in front of a flowering bush. It is tall and lush and green with purple cone-shaped flowers. A world of green lawn and blue sky. The apple blossoms are white, covering the trees like an infection and filling the air with sweet perfume. I am small, five years old. We have just moved to Newcastle and the old house is behind me, white and faded clapboard and a summer porch. I laugh with nostalgia but my five-year-old self is shaking his arms wildly in ecstatic wonder. I remember I would do this often as a child. It felt so good. I would build up this energy and then release it. I would shake my hands until I floated up to the edge of myself.

A big kid on a bike comes down the street and stops to watch me. He has red hair and freckles and is laughing at me.

"What the fuck is wrong with you, kid?" he asks me.

And that is the question I will be asking myself for the rest of my life. What is wrong with me? As a dead person I am asking myself, What was wrong with me?

What is that? Is it shame? I ponder. I was ashamed of everything: myself, my family, my body. My whole life was spent burying shame or trying to mask it. There was goof shame and athlete shame and student-council-president shame and sex shame and job shame and church-leader shame and parental shame and being-ashamed-of-being-here-in-this-life shame.

I remember reading a book where it said if we did not have mirrors, we would only know ourselves as arms, legs, feet and hands. We would never know what we looked like. We would only know what others looked like. Try it sometime. You feel a lot more. You become much more aware of everything. You think of yourself less. You notice the other, which is not you.

Don and I are back at the church.

"God will teach you to feel," Don says.

"I need to be given an instruction manual," I answer Don and laugh.

"Oh yes, God will teach you to feel." I hear a deep voice with a British accent. Not an old voice but a young voice with cadence.

"And guess who God is, Ronnie?" He says Ronnie like Ronneh with a rise on the eh.

"It's you!" And I hear a room full of laughter. "It's you it's you it's you!" The laughing voices chime until the room fills with the noise of them shouting "it's you!" I know the voice. It's Mick Jagger.

29

And then I hear another voice, a voice I recognize. "It's you, it's you." The voice jumps all over Jagger's. That voice is mine but I'm not talking.

This reminds me of a Bowie song that was remixed with clapping as the percussion, starting with one clap of hands and then overdubbed and overdubbed until it is a universe of clapping hands with electronics and Bowie's voice layered over, singing, "What have you done?" And that's what this is like, layers of voices, mine and his, and then the Bowie song comes in and Bowie sings "what have you done?" and the other voice says "it's you, it's you" and my voice says "it's you, it's you" and the clapping is filling everything like a thousand geese taking flight, flapping, flapping, clapping, clapping, and then a room appears.

A white room like in Kubrick's Odyssey, white and black squares for a floor and white walls and two chairs with bent black iron for legs and a table with black iron legs and a round white tabletop, and on one of the chairs in a white suit with white pointed shoes and a long white cigarette holder holding a cigarette that gently spirals smoke with one leg crossed sits Mick Jagger.

"Ronnie," he says and laughs, the *heh heh heh* laugh I have listened to hundreds of times on the El Mocambo recording, with the big Jagger grin with the wide mouth and the big teeth and the lips that could fit an Ethiopian as well as this skinny Englishman.

"Hi," I say. "Fancy meeting you here. Where the hell am I?"

"You're in your head," Mick says and taps the cigarette end off while he looks at it pondering something. He looks up. "You're not in the head you knew as your head. You're in your dreams which come from your big head."

"Oh," I answer. Jagger is shaking with small convulsive chuckles. He gets up and goes to a cupboard I did not notice before.

"Have a chair, Ronnie," he says. He takes two glasses out and returns, placing them on the table. He goes back and returns holding a crystal carafe with a golden liquor inside.

"I brought some whisky. I know you love whisky," Mick says. He pours each glass a third full. The glasses are cut crystal and reflect the light in prisms. I look for the light source but there isn't one. The place is light. If I look closely I can see sparkly jewels of light in everything.

I take a sip of the liquid. My nostrils, my throat, even my ears tingle and burn while I hold the liquor in my mouth. I swallow and relax. The heat of the slow movement down my throat relaxes my chest, my back. I realize my eyes have closed.

"That's wonderful," I say, opening my eyes to see him.

Jagger just nods and takes a sip of his own, pursing his lips with pleasure.

I am relaxed, so relaxed. I stretch out my legs and reach back over my head, clasping my hands behind my neck.

"How do you feel?" Mick asks.

"Wonderful. Just wonderful," I answer. "It's surprising meeting you here. I was expecting Jesus." I take another sip.

"I am your inner being," Mick says. "Everyone has an inner being, and we, your inner beings, can assume any form we want. And because we have access to all inner beings who have ever existed, we can do a pretty good job at emulating who we want to be. You see? Mick Jagger was so prominent and such an excellent representative of what we wanted to communicate to you that we assumed him very easily. Plus, it's fun being me." He mock bows and spreads his hands before me.

"Let's move to someplace more comfortable," he says, standing and moving to two large-backed lounge chairs, just like the ones in the Bose commercial. We both sit facing each other with a distance between us of about ten feet.

"Take another sip. Relax," he says to me.

I do. I am getting high. Everything becomes a little removed, a little distanced.

"Any questions?" Mick asks.

"Yeah. I must have royally fucked up."

"That's a statement, not a question," Mick answers and chuckles. Those Jagger eyes always look stoned, soft lids half closed and the smile, boyish and mischievous. Then he starts laughing and laughing, laughing so hard that other Micks start popping out of him until the room is full of Micks all laughing. It's too funny and I start laughing. Like the laughter on LSD where your head feels like it is popping popcorn. I have my eyes closed because I am trying to catch my breath and stop laughing and when I open them the room is full of dozens of me as my fifty-five-year-old self. I find I can jump my consciousness around from one to another, each looking at the others from another perspective. We are all dressed in suits that change colour with all the colours blending in and out of the suit. And then I look at myself in the chair and I am myself in the chair looking at Mick.

"How's that for fun?" Mick says.

"That's a gas, man," I say and watch all the others walk away into the light that surrounds us.

"It's like that, you know."

"Like what?" I answer.

"You create selves as easy as that. You go crazy when you first find out what you are capable of. Then you slow down when you realize they are all your responsibility."

"What do you mean? Do I have to keep an eye on them like a bunch of kindergarten kids?"

"They are only your responsibility in a way. Because they are all free agents of themselves. We all are. But they are parts of you, and you are the one they will come to for guidance and assistance. Another drink, Ronnie?"

I pass the glass with a stretched hand. Mick returns with it half full.

"Then you realize it's better just to have a few around to look after so you stop making them so often." He looks at his glass, cut crystal with honey liquid. I am watching intently.

"It's good to be immersed in reality, you know, the hardtack bones-and-mortar stuff. We all want to be there. But you forget once you're there that here even exists. That is where we do the work, really. We must be reminding them all the time that the hardtack bones and mortar is just as much air and fluff as this place is. So that they don't take themselves or it too seriously."

He looks at me and smiles.

"The catch is, the more seriously you take the other place the more fun life is, the more dramatic the journey. Because it's all about feeling, Ronnie. The more you feel, the better it is."

"But feelings are overwhelming."

"Yes," Mick says. "But feel this place and compare it. You miss the rage and the serenity of the blood, Ronnie. We try and keep you in the game for as long as possible. Everyone makes the exit on purpose. Every death is a suicide, so to speak. You say that's it, I've had enough, and together we plan an exit strategy. We all exit in a way to help others discover more depths to themselves."

"And what about the really horrible shit? Like Vietnam and the torture chambers?" I ask him.

"Choice. It's all choice, Ronnie. From here it's choice. From there it seems to be something else. But from here it's always choice. And there is a development of everything that is coalescing into a grand scheme. A lot of the horrible stuff is like a group of volunteers. They go to show humans what they don't want. It gets very complicated. And in a way suffering is just suffering. My advice is to learn to avoid it as best you can."

He smiles and looks intently at me.

"Rich Stadium 1978. I set this up at that concert. All your life from that point on I was very involved," Mick says with a grin.

"What about before that?" I ask.

"Before that it was your father."

"Were you around during those years?"

"Oh yes." Mick chuckles again. "I was always finding ways to give you strange metaphysical experiences. And I was always trying to show you beauty and contradiction, paradox. So that you could develop a sense of humour about Earth and the universe. And people, especially about people."

"Beauty and contradiction produce humour. How beautiful," I say with a smirk and a look at the tile.

"Yes, Ronnie. That's my invention. I had the most beautiful women in the world. And I was the contradiction. And it was funny. It was funny as hell." He looks into my eyes and leans forward, points with his Mick Jagger finger and shakes it, pushing his hips into his famous pucker. "Don't go into it too deeply or you'll ruin the fun." He sits back in the chair and relaxes. "You took things so seriously, Ronnie. You took on so many burdens. But if you look at it, it made you unique. It made your life a real good one."

"That all came from my old man," I say.

"Yes, he was that way. You asked him to be that way. Before you left to go and become human again you asked him. We take on roles like actors when we are planning those lives. But when we get there it's all fucking random. It all comes unglued. We forget everything and go nuts. That's what is so fucking fantastic about it."

"So reincarnation is a fact?" I ask.

"Ronnie. The universe is made up of stories that have been running forever. And they have been split up into billions of stories. And all the stories are running. And we kind of choose a theme or a storyline and jump in. Then we get born and we live out the story."

"Can we change the story?" I ask.

"A little. In each story there is a chance to see the light, as they say. Or to gain enlightenment. It's kind of what you did. You become aware of the story by stepping out of it and looking in at yourself. That's what it's all about. Because that is the beginning of a new game."

"What new game?" I ask, leaning forward. Mick leans to the side, angling his head loosely, closing his eyes.

"If you're here, Ronnie, you can't be there. If you're there, you can't be here. The two are mutually exclusive. It's like two minds. A mind creates this and another mind creates that. And you don't get to go there because of any merit or advancement. It's not like that. It's a calling. And when someone is called, it's everyone's job to get them past this and get them into the other mind. Into the mind of there."

He sits up straight and places his palms on his lap. "You remember your cousin said you'd been called?"

"Yes."

"He and I are helping you. It's our job to help you soar past the eagle. The eagle is your old mind that wants to keep you static. The eagle rules the earth because everyone wants to stop the world spinning. Everyone wants to stay as they are. But the game is evolution, transformation. It's like learning to fly without wings. It's impossible but it's not." He makes a flat hand gesture like a plane gliding.

"How?" I ask.

"We are to make you into a divine being. A divine being that maintains the human form."

"What's that supposed to look like?" I ask, sitting back and shaking my head.

"Don't worry," Mick says. "You won't be the miracle-working Jesus, if that's your concern." He stops and purses his lips. "Forget I said that. You might. But"—he points in the air—"you will become love, unconditional love. You will become divine in the sense that your big fat human ego will not be shitting all over everyone because you can't get your own way." He eyes me from a twisted-neck look. "That's the devil you know." He winks and smiles, the heavy-lidded Jagger smile.

"Humans with their big fat egos want everyone else to perform for them so they can have what they want. And what they don't know, Ronnie, is that everyone around them is a spirit actor on a stage doing exactly the opposite." His voice is rising and his jaw holds a grim posture of his mouth, which emphasizes mock seriousness.

"Because, Ronnie, if we all did what you wanted you would never sail anywhere. You would be trapped in your dumb ego fantasy forever."

He sits back and sips his drink.

"You, my friend, are going to end up loving everyone and all things the way God, dare I say, loves everyone and all things the same."

"But in the Bible it says God loved Jacob but hated Esau," I stammer. "It's tough hearing all this. It's rocking the root of me. It's shaking the glimmer out of me."

"God loves. Remember your epistle of John, Ronnie? God is love with no variance. Always love, nothing else." He pauses. "From here we love, Ronnie. We love all beings but especially humans. We were all humans. You could call us the advanced ones. There are not many of us. Only a few. We few, we happy few, we band of brothers. For he today who sheds his blood with me shall be my brother, be he ne'er so vile, this day shall gentle his condition."

"Henry the Fifth," I say.

"Your favourite?"

"Yes," I answer.

"You will help yourself become a beautiful creation, Ronnie, because humanity is a garden and the flesh is the soil and the hatred, disease, war and death are the fertilizer and the love of family and the love of the stranger and the love of the earth and the love of the spirit are the flowers that garden produces. We are the gardeners tending the tender shoots, bringing them up into the light. Then they leave us, and that is what we exist for, Ronnie, to send them off. You will leave and it will be magical and wondrous."

30

"And you get to stay here?" I ask Mick. "You're my inner being and you get to stay but I have to float away into the mist of eternity."

"You see, Ronnie, I don't want to go anywhere. This is where the fun is. I don't know what is beyond and I don't care. It's built into the being that I am. Just as to soar beyond the eagle is your being's raison d'être. Don't get the wrong impression. There are no greater or lesser beings. There are just beings, and when you get out of the ego pants you've been living in all these years you realize that we all fit into a grand scheme and our place in that scheme is our reason for being. You're here to suck the energy of your experiences like you would suck the marrow from a bone, so you can soar."

"So what now?" I ask Mick and sip my whisky.

"First memory," Mick says and snaps his fingers.

"Me and brother Rob. Hugging and holding each other and looking at our parents who have been screaming at each other like someone is going to die. And my mom saying, Oh Ron, look at the kids."

"Little Ronnie, eh?" Mick says. "Life is a shit storm. What do you feel when you look at that?"

I grunt. It comes from deep inside. "I feel helpless. I feel pain in my middle around my spine. I feel like everything is wrong and I feel like I want to die."

"You're feeling the whole lifetime of that emotion. It's like a well. Drawing on that first memory exposes the whole well of emotions that are connected to all experiences you suffered of that type. But one is all we need. Feel the emotion, whatever it is, fear, despair, feel it in your body and keep feeling it until it dissipates."

"But this isn't my real body," I say to him.

"No, it's your energetic body, but that is where emotional energy is caught. Release it here you release it everywhere, doing everyone a big favour."

"Okay," I say. I wait and feel. Thoughts start coming of temper tantrums and depression.

"Stop the thoughts!" the limey-accented voice shouts. "Don't let thoughts come. Feel the feelings. Feelings produce thoughts, not the other way around. That is the human thing. You indulge your emotions by thinking up stories. Just feel, Ronnie. Just feel."

I wait and feel. I feel the back of my throat constrict. I feel my forehead tighten and my shoulders tense. I sweat. I feel cold. I grit my teeth. It's a rush of heat and fever. I focus on the feelings. And gradually the tensions diminish, and I shiver and relax.

"And how do you feel, Ronnie?" Jagger asks.

"Fantastic. Like that Irish Spring commercial with all the naked people."

"Irish Spring?" Mick laughs and laughs again. He leans in toward the centre of us. "But really."

"Peaceful. Easy. I feel empty and full at the same time."

"That is what we must teach him," he says.

"Teach who?" I stammer.

"You, him, him, you," Mick answers, throwing a hand above his head.

"I'm dead."

"After all you've been through, you can't possibly believe that. You're still out there. The life you remember still exists. And you need to teach you so that your life will be lived the way you remember it."

"I teach him that emotion-without-thoughts thing?"

"Yes," Mick says. "That is the secret to living happily ever after."

"Really?" I say and fall back into the chair.

"Yes," Mick answers.

"Then why don't we all just learn that at the beginning and live happy forever? And how does that make us happy?"

"The answer to the first question is that humans are indulgent creatures. The answer to the second question is this: emotions carry thoughts. If you can experience an emotion and surrender it as you just did, the emotion becomes harmless. Just passing through." Mick makes a motion and a chuff chuff sound like he's pushing a model train between us.

"But if you add thoughts to the emotion the emotion continues and draws more energy to itself, and if it is a negative emotion, as most of them are, the emotion will become destructive because the thoughts it produces have power to destroy."

"So where do the emotions come from?" I ask him, looking askance like this is the stumper.

"They are inherent in DNA," Mick answers. "You were once primitive animals who used fear and flight as a means for survival. Then you became predators who used attack and killing as a means for survival. You use emotions for survival. You did not have the evolved consciousness you now have, so it worked. But now you are so complex. You can see what you feel."

"What the fuck?" I say and pound the arm of the chair and laugh.

Mick ignores me and continues like a professor in the middle of a lecture.

"Every threat you perceive as a human is the creek formed from the spring. And the spring is the fear of being eaten, fear of being attacked, fear of starving or the fear of whatever. You get it?"

"Yeah, yeah," I say.

"But now your minds have developed to a psychic awareness that can perceive new things. You can now transcend the fear of threat and attack. So to recognize where the threat stems from allows you to observe it without indulging it. And so you, we, he transcends the old indulgent human and become something else which remains to be seen." He lifts his eyebrows, looks at me and points. "In other words, you are what remains to be seen. And others like you, of course."

"Sounds like a fucked-up plan from the beginning," I say.

"How do you know?" he answers. "This is the plan. It is a huge fucking plan. This plan of evolved beings is so massive, so complex. You have no idea. And it's just getting started. Earth, puny little planet, is the beginning of something so incredible you cannot imagine."

I sit. I ponder with a spirit knuckle against my spirit mouth.

"And how do I begin?" I ask.

"We look for a place in your past where we can insert you. He in your earth body and you in an ethereal body. We will put you where he is. He will need to be in an altered state, which is normal for him because he has a drug problem."

"Oh yeah," I say. "Like the Indians would get their apprentices to take peyote."

He shakes his head. "Yes, it is like that. But altered states can be states of beauty, you know. Let's do a trial run. Imagine a beautiful time."

"Okay, I remember standing at a horse farm watching the western sky. It was huge there and the sun would play with the clouds, creating amazing colour. Blue and orange streaks, wisps of molten egg yolk yellow, like an abstract, and my wife sneaks up and smacks me between the shoulders, like in the Castaneda books where Don Juan would hit Carlos between the shoulder blades to move his assemblage point and put him in heightened awareness."

Mick laughs. "That was a very funny thing for your wife to do. So abrupt, so physical and a joke totally restricted to the two of you. No one else would know what the fuck she was doing or why you were laughing."

"It's true, man. We would laugh at the same things, talk about the same things. We had the same sense of humour. We were really quite bold. I miss that. I miss her."

"Look," he says.

And I look.

31

I stand on the earth. The summer earth, hard and dry. And there's the smell of horse shit and dust. And I have my arm around my wife. We are big people, solid, with our jodhpurs and boots. The tall trees shake their leaves and make air noise and the sky, oh the sky. I love the sky. Oh, how I love the sky and the birds shooting from tree to pole. I had forgotten. I had forgotten. I long for this place. Oh my god, how I long for this place.

"You see how easy it is," he says. I am sitting across from him once again.

"I have never felt longing like that," I say.

"Good, good," he says. "Longing is good. But for now, we must find him in a desperate place. Think about a time, Ronnie. Think about being scared. Fear is good. Especially irrational fear."

"I know, man. I've got it. There was this weekend. I was with this chick and we snorted dust. It was good. I remember I liked it. I knew I was frying my brain but I had given up on myself. You know, like I had decided I was going to dope and drink myself to death and I did not care."

"Why?" Mick asks. "Why didn't you care?" I look up and he is sitting forward with an elbow on his knee and a fist supporting his chin.

"I was a loser. I had failed. Everyone had lost faith in me."

"Who specifically?" Mick asks.

I look down at my hands to answer. "Everyone. My dad, my coaches, my teachers, even my friends didn't want me around much. My mom was ashamed of me. My parents had stopped going to my hockey games because I would fight so much. And then I punched the ref. That was after my grandfather died. I would drive Mom every day that summer to look after him. He was bedridden in the house and I guess watching him fade into nothing, into a yellow skeleton with skin, was too much for me. My parents were probably preoccupied. They were probably unable to cope with that. But I was on a tragic slide, for sure."

"What was it like being you then?" His voice is coming as if from far away, but I look and he is still there, opposite me.

"I was a goof. I would get so out of it. Girls despised me. I was very alone. That was how it felt. So alone, Mick."

"Feel it, Ronnie. Feel it. Stop thinking now and just feel. Feel until there are no feelings. Let the emotions dissipate. Can you see yourself?"

And it's like I am in a plane, looking down through clouds and there I am, sitting on Main Street, Newcastle, on a bench in front of the town hall. I look up at the clock tower and it is ten p.m.

"What do you see yourself doing?" Mick asks.

"I am blasted. I can see that," I answer. "I can see that by the way the head falls at the neck, pivots front to back and side to side."

I see a truck pull up. "That's my friend Brock's truck," I say. "It's a dark-gold Chev four-by-four pickup, you know, the ones with the locking hubs, the old four-wheel drives."

"Keep looking, keep describing," Mick says.

The truck pulls up and the window rolls down. Music is blaring out of the cab.

"Do you hear, Mick? Do you hear? It's Dancing with Mr. D. It's the Goats Head Soup album. It's you singing, man."

I hear Brock call to me. "Hey Moose, what ya doin'? C'mon with us."

I get up, get in and Brock's friend Murph moves over to make room. It's a bench seat and our elbows rub. The dash lights are milky because of the angel dust.

"I can't see too well," I say to myself.

"Holy fuck, Moose, you're already ripped," Brock says with a laugh and accelerates onto the road. "Wanna get more ripped? We have some blue microdot."

Murph produces some foil and gently unfolds it and wets a finger and holds it before me. I can't see the blue specks.

"There's a few there, Moose." I lick my finger and touch it to his and peek intently until I see them. I lick them off and Murph passes me a beer from a small cooler between our feet on the floor to wash them down. It's cold and the liquid hits my throat like a shock of carbonated ice. The bottle is an experience in my hand. I can't tell how hard I am holding it. It feels like I am going to drop it or squeeze it until it breaks. Then it feels jagged and sharp. I look to see if it is shattered but it's still a bottle in my hand.

"We're going to the big hill, Moose," Brock is saying. He has a square chin and long features like Superman. I look at Murph with his beard and his red hair and think he looks like one of Robin Hood's merry men. He is saying something and laughing but I can only think or hear or talk, one at a time.

Gimme Shelter comes on the speakers. It sounds milky, but it is soothing. I start to move in my seat.

"You like that, eh Moose?" Brock asks. "I put all my Stones on this eight track but randomly so all the songs are mixed."

"Like a greatest hits," I say. "I was just with Mick Jagger." I can hear Mick laughing somewhere in the background.

"Oh yeah, Moose," Brock says, laughing. Murph is laughing too.

"You are fucking high," Murph chimes.

"If I fucking told ya, ya wouldn't believe me," I say and look out the window. I am not laughing because somehow the connection has been made. And I am back.

32

The truck vibrates with the rumble of the V8 engine. Mick is singing Love in Vain on the speakers. The bluesy acoustics are soothing and I start singing.

"Moose, stop," Murph says. "You're starting me tripping and it can't be the acid kicking in so soon." Brock laughs and pounds the steering wheel with the palm of his hand.

We cruise north up paved roads boarded by fences and trees made visible by the headlights. No one talks. I wonder if they are getting off. Brock and Murph are dope veterans. You can barely tell when they're starting to get off. Then we turn in the dirt roads at Burketon and the truck bounces and I can feel my ass and legs bouncing off the seat. The smell is like my old man's grease gun as the engine guns us over the hills and down the paths. It smells like a taste: hard, bitter, burned friction, the end of the world in a volcano. All I see are trees. They seem to come out of the forest toward the truck, as if they were rushing toward us and not the other way around. The suspension of the truck is hard and throws us around in the cab. Brock is laughing and stoops as he drives with both hands on the wheel, like his vehicle is an animal that may get away from him if he doesn't hold it tight. Murph has both hands on the dash to steady himself. I have one on the dash and one gripping the door handle. Brock accelerates up the hills, sand dunes covered in long grass with tire trail carved into them, and then he coasts down, up and down with the engine growling in exertion and purring in release until we get to the bottom the hill.

It's all sand, rising at a steep angle that you would never think of climbing with a motorized vehicle, let alone a truck. At the top is a chute cut in where the successful bidders drive through in an explosion of sand and dirt. Brock stops and waits.

It is quiet. The only sound is the truck idling. It rocks us just a bit.

"Ready, Moose?" Brock asks.

I don't answer. I am off in reverie.

"Murph?"

"Give 'er," Murph replies, and instead Brock gets out and goes to each front wheel, casually, lighting a cigarette as he stands in the headlights before us. His tall bony frame in a white T-shirt and jeans, with boots and black hair like a six-foot-two Keith Richards. Somewhere in my fog of memory Brock is dead. It was a long time ago and it's still in the future. No one even told me. I found out from a cousin of his I knew through the horses. But there he is. "Fuck," I sigh.

Murph looks at me with a quiet eye.

"Forgot to lock the hubs," Brock calls.

"We wouldn't have got far in two-wheel drive," Murph comments, still looking at me. Murph knows something. Maybe he's from the future too. I'm so stoned I want to grab him and shake him. "Why didn't you look after Brock?" But I'm so stoned I don't.

"No, that's for sure, Murph, that's for sure," Brock says, getting back in the cab.

Murph moves his knees against mine so Brock can pull the shift into four-wheel. And then he drops the shift on the column into low. "Hang on, Moose," he says and I think I hear empathy. Someone told me Brock died from drug use. I never spoke to anyone about it. Murph became a born-again Christian like me. Murph grabs my hand and shakes it, palm over wrist, like he knows. My blurred vision focuses ahead on the hill.

"Ready boys?" Brock asks and looks straight ahead. From where we are we cannot see the top of the big hill, just a wall of red and brown dirt that rises. And then the roar of the engine, the torque on the frame and the pull of the tires and the lights accelerating onto and up the steep incline. The sand is flying past my open window and the truck starts rabbit hopping. It fishtails to the right and the left with Brock wrestling the steering wheel to correct it and keep us straight. But one fishtail catches and throws the truck sideways and I am looking out my window at the hill which is now below me, almost close enough to touch.

It smells of fresh-tilled soil, of when I worked on sod farms cutting the earth in the dew-fresh mornings. It smells of my grandmother's garden which I would hoe and weed when I was a kid. I notice a shadow. The moon has appeared and the truck silhouette is cast upon a silvered ground.

"Keep your arms in, Moose," Brock says. "We're pretty close to rolling."

Murph grabs me under the arm. "I've got ya, Moose."

Brock manoeuvres the vehicle, gunning the engine and spinning the tires while cranking the wheel. He keeps repeating this, each time backing a little farther down the hill. At one point we are so erect that I cannot see over the hood. But again and again, Brock corrects the position until we are straight and he can back all the way down.

At the bottom Brock turns the truck and faces away from the hill, puts it in park and says, "Let's get out and smoke a joint."

"Nice driving," Murph says.

"Eh Moose?" he adds, looking at me.

"Oh yeah," I say and turn to look at the hill. In my vision it has separated into two hills. One is like a reflection in silver, but it is raised above the brown sand. I look around and there are two of everything. There are two Brocks, two Murphs, two trucks, everything in silhouette.

"I think I'm getting off," I say. Brock passes me a joint and I toke and pass it to Murph. I feel no effect, but when the joint comes back around I take it and draw on it. But still no effect. I look around and everything is distorted.

"Let's go," Brock says.

Murph goes to the truck. "You sit in the middle this time, Moose."

"Sure," I say and move to the open door. I must move by feeling. Feeling my feet touch the earth. Feeling my hand touch the door. Feeling my feet on the floor of the truck and my ass on the bench seat. Because my eyesight is fucked. I am seeing many waves and shapes in the dark, and as the truck moves out onto the path I can see people in the trees.

"You're with him now," I hear Mick's voice say. It's a voice in my head but it's clear and distinct. "Breathe and feel his emotions. Don't think anything about them. Just feel and release."

"I see two hills," I hear myself say. "One is close and one is getting far off."

"You must be really getting off," Murph says to me.

"Were you already high when we picked you up, Moose?" Brock asks me.

"I have never been this high," I answer.

I look at Brock. He head has extended like a totem. His features become strange, unidentifiable.

"Focus him," I hear Mick, my inner voice, say. So I do. I remember Brock as I knew him, arm-wrestling, tall, angular Brock. And his hallucinated image relaxes back into itself.

We drive and drive, with the music, the lights, everything low and soft, with Brock talking. I can't understand him. He's telling a story to Murph and Murph is laughing. I watch out the window. The trees are stiff in the headlights. The road is a worm that pulls us. Bugs are bullets of light that swerve. We slow and turn and speed up. The truck talks with vibrations. We climb a hill and turn into a lane. We pull up to a house, get out and I follow them inside.

Moose

My friends, OJ, Limey and Ted are there. They are playing a game called Rebound. It's a bright yellow plastic board with two elastics stretched at forty-five-degree angles. You push a brightly coloured puck with a loose ball bearing in its centre up and off the elastics and down the other side to where there are lines and numbers. You score points for how accurate you can place the puck in those numbered areas, like shuffleboard. The only problem for me is that the pucks are forming a solid line, a trail of blue and pink and red. People are talking and I can hear my name but I can't understand anything.

"Get him alone," Mick shouts in my head. "Get him out of that room and away from that board."

The upstairs of OJ's house is unused and full of old clothes and blankets on a bed. I know because I have crashed here before.

"OJ," I say. "Can I go upstairs for a bit? I am freaking out."

"Moose is on acid," I hear Murph say.

"And dust," I add.

"Okay," OJ says. "Don't freak out." He laughs. The other three laugh. I am a laughingstock. I have been in the habit of getting too high, too drunk and becoming an asshole. I am a liability. Someone to be taken care of. Shame rises up. What a fucking loser. You could have amounted to something. But here you are, a fucking drugged-out piece of shit. These thoughts cover my head like a cone of iron.

"Those are his feelings," Mick says. "Stop adding thoughts of your own. Just feel and release."

"I'll be okay," I say to the guys and head for the stairs. It's dark but the dark is a refuge from the light. The stairwell is narrow and my hands touch each side, guiding me. I get to the top and sit on the bed. It is piled with clothes and blankets that smell of mothballs. I fall into them, like falling into someone's past. OJ's dad had just died. His dad was a lot older than his mom. Everyone loved OJ's dad. He had tight curly grey hair that made him look like Arlo Guthrie. His mom was cool too. She would let us party and she would make these buns with cheese and bacon when we got the munchies. He had lost a brother who got hit by a car on the 115 when we were just little kids. That must have been tragic. No wonder he thinks I'm a joke. People who have really suffered don't understand the mock suffering of losers.

"Turn on the TV," Mick says.

My dead self remembers this. The old black and white TV with bunny ears is on a stand at the end of the room. I remember doing this the first time and watching the Three Stooges in black and white. The TV is old and takes a while to warm up. It's a time warp up here, my dead self thinks, a black and white TV in a room full of memories and watching the Three Stooges. It's perfect. I feel something rebirthed in myself, an awareness of myself as a watcher of things, a noticer of coincidence and beauty. Because this attic is beautiful. But the drugs are so strong.

I turn on the TV. And sure enough, a Three Stooges movie is playing.

"You can talk to him now," I hear Mick say.

"Pardon?" I say.

"Go into the TV," Mick says, "and talk to him. He is awakening and you are the missing link between him and me, between him and his inner being."

"And how does someone go into a television show?"

"Imagination, Ronnie. It's how we do everything. You just aren't aware of it yet. But imagination is the creator of everything. So think about the Stooges. Think about one of them in particular."

And so I think about Curly, big bald Curly with his anxiety antics. His *woop woop woops* and his standing on his toes and twirling. "Every time I hear that weasel something pops out of me," I say in a high scratchy voice. And I am looking out of the TV at myself buried under blankets in the dark. I can only see my eyes peering out.

"Come on," I say from Curly. "Get a grip on yourself. What ya hidin' fo'?" I do a tippy-toe twirl and tap the top of my bald head with my palm at the back, like my fingers are the visor of a hat.

But freaked-out druggy me doesn't move, stays hidden.

"What's up with him?" a much shorter than I am Moe says, coming up beside me and pointing out the screen at the guy under the covers.

"Beats me," I say from Curly's voice.

"If we had some birdseed we could lure him out of his nest," Larry says, coming up beside me.

"He's human, ya numbskull. He ain't no bird," Moe says, looking at Larry with disgust.

"But he's got a bird brain," I say and Moe brings his fists in a reverse arm spiral and knocks both me and Larry on the back, me because I made the comment and Larry because he thinks it's funny.

"I must be really fucking out of it if the TV is talking to me," I hear my drugged-out self say from under the covers.

"This is your chance, big guy," Moe says.

"Yeah, he's listening," Larry says.

I step forward as Curly, preen myself like an opera singer and say in the high screechy voice, "You gotta stop this. You have a good life ahead of you. It's important. I know you're very lonely, but there is a time coming and soon where you will never be lonely again."

"I don't believe that," my under the covers self says. "My life is a waste. I hate it. I hate myself. I just fucking want it to end." He throws the covers off and pushes himself up off the bed and stands looking at the TV and us. His hair is long, hanging down past his shoulders and he has a big beard that covers his neck. He's overweight but I smile like he's a child I have not seen for too long and I smile and Moe and Larry put their arms over my shoulders on each side.

"He's a real beauty," Larry says.

"Yeah," Moe adds. "You should be proud."

"Thanks guys," I answer as Curly, soaking in the praise.

"I am fucking out of it," druggy me says and exits the room.

"Follow him," Mick says fervently, adamantly.

"I'm stuck in a TV set," I say as Curly and laugh. "There is too much levity here, in this black and white world. I can't take myself serious anymore."

I can hear Mick laughing. "That is one of the lessons you are learning on behalf of all of us."

"What's that?" Curly asks as I stand outside the TV.

"Not to take things so seriously," Mick says.

"Oh, we know that already," Larry says from beside Curly.

"See ya, kid. It was nice havin' ya," Moe says and I reach down and turn off the TV.

33

"Follow him," Mick says again. "You have a body again but no one can see you. You are like a ghost to them."

"Can I do tricks and freak them out?" I ask.

"Yes, but you don't have time. Get after him."

"Okay," I say with a whine because I am having too much fun. I go down the stairs and slide through the door without moving it too much. He is standing at the table, watching the stupid game.

"Feeling better, Moose?" OJ asks.

"Yeah, a bit. I'm going for a walk."

"Whatever, Moose," OJ comments without looking.

I follow myself out the door and up by the barn. The night is breezy and the sky is stars partially obscured by clouds. The long grass rises on each side of a tractor path he walks down. I follow. The hills of Kirby drop off around us, smooth contours rolling into valleys. Geese are squawking and raising a ruckus in the cornfield beside us. The corn is tall and dry and leaves rattle against each other with the breeze. I smell the dirt and the grass, the brown and the green while the trees above us catch the air with whispers.

I look for him and he is on the ground, on his back rolling from side to side, clutching himself in an embrace. He is moaning. "No, no. Go away. Leave me alone."

"What's wrong with him?" I ask.

"It's fear, Ronnie. It's got him."

"Who are you? Why are there so many of you? Leave me alone!" he yells from the ground.

"What the hell, Mick. What do I do?"

"Go over and put your hands on him."

I walk to him. It's weird watching myself succumb to emotion like this.

"His friends are right. He's a suck. He's repulsive," I say to Mick.

Mick laughs. "You don't like this. Grow up. This is the beginning of his release."

I stoop and put my hands on his shoulders. I can only place them lightly because I am very light. But terror seizes me, it takes over, paralyzing fear. Pictures of lying in the bed in Newcastle while our dad screamed at our mom. Feelings of being powerless to do anything. Noises from the basement in the middle of the night, wood splitting and hammering. Our mother crying while my brother and I curl under the covers in fear. He curls into himself now and I can feel his hatred for himself, that he didn't do anything to help his mom. That he was a coward all his life. It passes through me, the emotions, like electric currents. I become a passive conduit. He relaxes, stretches out on the path. I stand.

"Who the fuck are you?" he says.

He is looking at me and I realize he can see me.

"I'm you," I answer. "Come to help you."

I watch him stand to his feet.

"What happened there?" I ask him.

"Never mind," he says.

"I can tell you," I say. "You thought the geese were people, like people of the corn. You thought they were demons coming to take your soul. You were hallucinating and you thought they were screaming."

"How do you know?"

"I been through this once."

"The big spin," he says.

"Millson," I answer.

"You know that? Millson's spin theory?"

"I never forgot it," I say. "I've repeated a few things. You get a bit deeper into them every time. Until you get to the bottom or the top. It's kind of inverted."

"So last time, did someone like you turn up to help you?" he asks.

"Probably," I say. "But I don't remember it very well. How do you feel?"

"Still really high, but all the paranoia and freak-out are gone."

"What now?"

"I'm walking home."

"That's probably ten miles."

"I've done it before."

And he pauses, looking at the ground. "That bit that Curly said from the TV, that I would be happy and have a good life. Is that true?"

"You really can't imagine," I say. But I hear Mick's voice in my head say, "Don't tell him too much. You've said enough."

"Yes, it's true," I say. "But I can't say too much."

"Okay," he says, smiling. "I heard the other voice too. I'll see ya. I've got to walk this shit out of my system. And talking to you is too weird. It's freaking me out all over again."

He walks away from me, down the path. I follow and watch him walk past the barn and down the gravel drive. Not a word to his friends in the house, not a word to anyone. He walks out of my sight.

"Tender is the night," Mick recites beside me.

He stops in front of me with his smile that starts at his chin and ends at his eyes. He glimmers with joy. I am smiling too.

"That was a trip," I say.

"Yes 'twaz sir, yes 'twaz."

"It was weird. That emotion of fear went so deep, it traumatized him. It has traumatized him—me, for my entire life."

Mick is still in his white suit with his long-toed white patent-leather shoes.

"No, it hasn't," Mick says, stomping the gravel. "Man, I love the earth. I haven't been here for a while." And he stomps and jumps. "It's the hardness of it, Ronnie. Gravity and all that. It really is miraculous."

"But what about the trauma? What about the fear and his inner shudder of helplessness?"

Mick stops and looks at me. "I'll let you in on a secret, Ronnie." He comes up close to me. "Everything is a metaphor. Every event, every moment is a metaphor for something else. But while in your earth body it is very elusive." He stops, looks up at the big willow in the yard. "You can get it from beyond the body, because that is what is happening with you, with us. We are getting it."

"Getting what?"

He turns and faces me again. "That none of this is real. It is all based on ideas. It's like trying on ideas. Everyone needs an engine to propel them through this life. That fear is our engine. It kept you moving until you got to me. And every life is different, not just a little different. You humans think that you're all alike. Poppycock. You are all as different as one galaxy from another. Don't get me wrong. It is necessary. It all works but you imagine it wrong. Every one of us is a separate universe. And as you can see, each one of us is many."

"So how do you sort that out?" I say.

Mick laughs, a snort and a snicker toward the ground.

"Isn't that the thing, Ronnie? Humans always sorting it out. Judging this and that, forever and ever and on and on. But it's futile. It's immense, it's out of our range of understanding. We cannot reach the place where there is an understanding."

"It just seems wrong."

"What?" Mick asks. "What seems wrong?"

"Suffering. Like what I suffered was nothing. It seems so overblown, my reaction to it. Yelling and fighting and my old man always on my case and all that shit. It's small potatoes. Look what it did to me. It destroyed me and it was nothing. Some people are sexually molested, tortured, beaten, children in wars and, holy fuck, Mick. You know what I am saying."

"I know what you are saying," Mick answers me. "And like I said before, humans are indulgent creatures. They take every story and dramatize it and replay it and squeeze it for every bit of emotional juice. News on the BBC, ABC, CBC, the Arabs and the Russians all playing the same stories for the world to read, watch and hear. I am not saying that the things you mention don't happen. But that is not your job. You can't fix the world. There are people born for that. You have been called to something else."

"What, then?" I say.

"Right there, with your Moose self. You felt his suffering as emotion. You did not judge it, you did not indulge it, you released it from him back to its source. And that is what you are going to do and what you are going to teach him to do, and he is going to teach others to do."

"Just that?" I say. "Just that little idea. That's nothing."

"It's not nothing," Mick answers angrily, his voice sharp. "When you release that energy, that emotion of fear, you are draining a well, his well of fear, but you also release the fear of someone or many someones on the planet as well. That child who is suffering finds a release. The drunk, the prostitute, the workaholic, the sexaholic, the war monger, all the ones societies avoid. They hold that energy for a reason. It's to be released." His voice softens. "It's very big, Ronnie. And many are doing the same thing. The great prophets and teachers, they are doing this. They do it quietly. They do it in secret. Very few of them are known. Some gain recognition so they can teach others, but they are insignificant to the total."

"Is the energy trapped here?" I say.

"You're on to it, Ronnie."

"Like for the evolution to move forward the energy of the past must be released. And by indulging it, we keep it cycling, over and over."

"I knew you were a bright one," Mick says mockingly.

"And does that energy recreate things of its own nature?" I ask.

"It does, it does, my friend. Have you ever heard the saying judge not lest you be judged?"

"King James Version. How appropriate for a limey," I say with a laugh.

"Yes, I remember you become a bit of a Bible scholar later on. But the man was right. Whatever you judge stays. Whatever you do not judge is released. It goes."

"So is karma just judging and re-judging and re-judging?"

"Lifetime to lifetime to lifetime," Mick chimes in.

"And are there forces behind all this?"

"You mean like demons?" Mick says abruptly, wide-eyed like it's preposterous to ask.

"Yes," I answer and wait.

He waits too, and a smile emerges.

"Yes. There are demons. You read about them later on in those Castaneda books."

"The flyers?" I say, screwing up my face.

"Yes, the big fat multidimensional things. They're hard to see, but once you see one you don't want to see them again." Mick screws up his face too and winces.

"I remember Carlos was horrified by them."

Mick nods with a sour look of lips pursed and squinty eyes.

"Are they aliens?"

"Sort of. We think they were sent to force this place to move on. Humans were kinda getting stuck, you know. Wars and greed and wealth and poverty, they have always existed as opposites, in a balance. But you guys have pushed this to the extreme. Those beings feed off negative energy, they feed like pigs at a trough. Most of the big players in your world are jumpers. They have managed to get a few of themselves into human form. They don't like to do it, changing form, because it takes too much energy and they are very slothful."

"Then what good are they?" I ask. I look around and the wind has picked up. I hear thunder in the distance.

"They will make you sick of yourselves. By that I mean your primitive ego selves, the ones governed by fear. Because fear ultimately produces all suffering."

"And is there a big finale where the angels and devils fight it out?"

"No, Ronnie. There's a big whimper where everyone says oh shit, I was wrong all along."

A storm flashes lightning close by. The sky blackens. Mick looks up and continues.

"But gradually you will all step out of yourselves and discover that you are all ultimately the same spirit, and that fear is not necessary, and that coexistence in love and peace is all that is real."

Mick is looking at the sky.

"And what will the flyers do then?" I ask him.

"They will leave. They will move on."

"And where will they go?" I ask.

"To borrow an expression from you, fucked if I know." Mick looks at me, compresses his lips and lifts his shoulders.

"And how long will it be until we learn and they leave?" I ask.

"Not as long as you think, Ronnie. Not as long as you think."

He looks up at the storm. The wind is ripping at the tall trees around us. The thunder cracks and ripples in crashes and murmurs. Hail strikes the ground around us but we are not solid enough for it to bounce off so it passes through us. Mick smiles and waves an arm, like he's forming a rainbow with gesture, and the storm subsides immediately.

"Was that the flyers?" I ask. "Causing the storm?"

"Yes," he answers. "But they've got nothing on us, so I sent them away."

"Cool," I say.

"Yes, Ronnie. One day you will do the same."

34

Mick looks down the road. "I hate it when you do that," he says.

"Who, me?" I answer.

"Not you, him," Mick says. "Wandering off like that, isolationist tendencies. He thinks being alone is the answer."

"It's not?" I say.

Mick turns on a heel and studies me. His right index finger presses his cheek up and he rests his elbow on his opposite hand.

"No, Ronnie. Being alone is never the answer. Jesus on the mountain and all that crap. You know where Jesus spent all his time?"

"Yes, I do," I answer. "At the home of Lazarus with Martha and Mary."

"And why?" His finger is poised to drop and point at me when the answer is given.

"Because they were rich and he could rest in comfort."

"Bingo," he says and lets the finger drop.

He looks back down the road where our subject is now walking alone toward his home.

"It takes an advanced spiritual being to know how to be alone," Mick says. "Most humans use their solitude to sulk, and I don't think he is any exception, do you?"

I chuckle to myself, thinking of how much sulking I had done in my life.

"You're right," I say.

"And you thought you were a spiritual being?" Mick asks, still staring into the distance.

Now I am laughing.

"The one is always many, Ronnie. What is around you is who you are. And as you move along your path what is around you will change. The others will change and become different. But they are all there to assist you. It may not be pleasant, and being pushed out of the mire and swamp of an indulgent ego is never easy. But once you are out and sailing free you never think of it. Once you're free you're free, and that is the reason for being here."

Mick fingers his cheek again and cocks one hip in a determined stance.

"All he does is get bombed and hang out with that old crowd."

"Yessiree," I answer. "And they're pretty fed up with him."

"Does he have any other friends?"

"You know," I say. "You're his inner being."

"Yes, but I'm thinking," Mick says, looking down the road to where our physical counterpart has vanished.

"Remember," I say, "he hangs out with Tit Shields every now and then."

Moose

"Yes," Mick says, turning on a heel. "And he has that experience."

"Yes, he has that experience," I say.

"You must be there when he has it. And we will strategically stage an event."

"But can we mess with history that way?"

Mick folds the skin on his forehead and turns his eye on me.

"Don't interrupt, Ronnie. Not when I am in the stages of brilliant invention."

"Okay," I say with a laugh. "You could have been a comic."

"I know," Mick says. "Like one of those Monty Python characters. But you are part of me, and alas I took myself too seriously as well. That's where you got it." Mick lowers his head as if to confide and speaks in a lowered tone.

"You should know by now: there is no past, there is no future. There is only what we are observing, and even then we are making that up. You can't interfere with anything because nothing exists."

"I'm afraid that sort of thinking will not fit in my pint-sized brain," I say.

"It's not your brain, Ronnie," Mick says, raising his head and turning again toward town. "You have a wrong interpretation. And as a result, he has a wrong interpretation. You have interpreted the life experience wrongly." He smiles.

"Did anyone ever tell you that you look like the Cat in the Hat?" I ask him.

"Yes. I'm sure that Dr. Seuss guy used my face as inspiration for that stupid cartoon. But stop the diversions."

"Okay," I say. "I don't think I have any interpretation of my life. I died and I am standing on the fifth line in the middle of the night with Mick Jagger."

"But Ronnie . . ." Mick turns and puts his palms in a prayer position before him. "He holds your thoughts and you think that your life is a fuck up, a shit storm, a haphazard blitzkrieg of randomness."

"But isn't that what it is?" I say.

"Yes," he answers, standing tall and turning away from me. "It is as you say, but you've got the colour wrong. You don't see the light. You only see the dark. C'mon, we're on the move."

"Okay," I say and follow Jagger, who has started walking at a brisk pace.

"It's a long walk to Newcastle," I say to him.

"We are spirits, Ronnie. Remember, the rules of time and place are not constraints on us."

35

He turns into a road allowance with a gate. He jumps over the gate and I follow. We walk into a stand of bush. There is a path with a black emptiness between the trees. I follow him into it and through it and we walk out of it onto Mill Street in the town of Newcastle opposite the house I grew up in.

"Here we are," Mick says. "And this is the night under consideration."

It's late. It's summer. I look up and the streetlight is surrounded by bugs that gyrate in excited patterns like some kind of an atomic machine. It's quiet. Too quiet.

"Why is it so quiet?" I ask Mick.

I hear my voice like it's another person's and it's tight and my teeth are chattering like a little kid just out of a swimming pool. Mick comes up and hits me with the bottom of a fist in the centre of my back between my shoulder blades. Warmth spreads through my body and I relax.

"Thanks, I needed that," I say, mimicking an old commercial.

Mick laughs too. "I remember that," he says. "Aqua Velva or something where a woman slaps a guy on the face after a shave."

"Yes, it was aftershave, like a cologne," I say, shaking my body. "What happened to me?"

"That doorway shook you up a bit," Mick says. "Passing through dimensions kinda shakes you up the first time. It gets easier."

"Where is everyone?" I say because I notice that we are the only people. Even if it is the middle of the night we should hear cars on the 401 or see an occasional car pass. But it is dead.

"Give it a moment, Ronnie," Mick says and points down the street. A blob like a black puffball is compressing itself into a pancake and pushing itself into a ball and then into an oblong water balloon in the air and then falling in a splat into a pancake again. It uses this change in shape to move itself down the street toward us. It moves down from the top of the 401 bridge. It doesn't move fast but takes pauses between each bounce as if it were out of breath. And on each landing it makes no noise in spite of its dimensions. It's huge. At rest it must be thirty feet in girth.

"Why is there no noise?" I ask Mick.

"The noise is in another dimension," he answers while he watches. "We are between worlds."

When the blob gets to us it blocks out the crosswalk sign completely. It's the full width of the road.

"That thing's hideous," I say to Mick as it passes heading north.

Mick just nods.

"Why can we see it?"

"Because our friend has taken mescaline. He is between worlds. We are going to see some things tonight. The flyer is the least dramatic. The most impressive, for sure, but the least dramatic."

Headlights approach from the south. The car engine and the tires make noise as they pass. I see people inside and then I hear the 401 sounds.

"Things are settling," Mick says. "Which way to your friend's?"

I point and proceed west, past the nursing home and toward the Shields' house.

"I think there will be quite a few girls at this party," Mick says as we walk.

"Yes, Tit is magical with girls." I look at him. "He's a lot like you," I say, laughing. "He's small, wiry and a great storyteller. He has curly hair that's thick like wool and he doesn't do anything that I can remember, no sports, no school stuff. He's just into girls."

"That's quite a contrast to our Moose," Mick says.

"Oh yes. He's terrified of girls," I answer, smirking to myself.

"And as we know he'll be shitting himself if one of those girls comes on to him," Mick says, striding along.

"And he's on mescaline."

"And that does not bode well for him, does it, Ronnie?"

"Not if I remember it correctly." I stop and point. "That's the house."

It's a yellow brick bungalow with a garage. The grass is long and uncut. Weeds grow randomly in spires of dried stalk. I can hear the muffled bounce of the stereo from inside. I can see someone move in the dark living room. There are no curtains.

"It looks like this is an abandoned house," Mick says.

"The mom left," I say. "It's only the dad and the four boys that live here. They're not much on landscaping. They're all free spirits."

"It's good," Mick says. "It's good to have that much freedom."

"I had enough freedom to get murdered. That's really cool."

"If that's what it takes."

I look at him and wince. "Whatever you say. This death thing has not been easy."

Mick nods but I notice a weariness in him, like my suffering has been his suffering.

We walk around the house and open an aluminum door with no glass or screen, just an aluminum doorframe painted yellow. We push open the wooden door behind it and enter the house. We can see people at the bottom of the basement stairs and we go down. The dampness settles on my skin. I smell cigarettes, perfume and the musky concrete. And beer. The place reeks of stale beer.

"Oh god," I say, "this place is—" but Mick stops me with a hand on my arm. He is looking up at me.

"Did you notice, Ronnie?" he says.

I stand back and pull my hands up in front of me as if they were in danger of being nipped.

"You look like a girl," I say. He has makeup and lipstick and eyeliner, and if I didn't know better I would think he was a woman.

Moose

"I don't just look like a woman," Mick says. "I am a woman." He leans into my face to speak. "And so are you, Ronnie."

"What?" I say, reaching for my crotch and my breasts.

"Oh my god," I say and laugh with a high-pitched giggle. Mick squeezes my arm.

"Keep yourself under control," he says, leaning into my ear as we cross the room.

The music is loud. Mountain is playing Mississippi Queen.

"That's your song, Ronnie. After all, you are a big girl," Mick yells, still leaning into me and pushing me along. The music is so loud you have to yell to be heard.

"Yeah," I yell back into Mick's ear. "Maybe I could use my new apparatus on Moose. Be his first fuck."

Mick grabs his girl nose and laughs, stumbling and almost pulling me down. I lift him up by the armpit. He takes my arm to stand up. He is a full head shorter than I am, in a halter and shorts and rope sandals. He's cute.

I can't imagine what I look like. I feel agile and quick. I feel like getting in a fight. I feel girl tough. I'm looking around. Mick's arm is tight on mine.

"No, no, no, no, no," she says. "Stay with the program."

"Remember the 3rd Rock from the Sun show?" I ask him.

"Of course. I'm you, remember, and you are going to tell me that you think you are like Sally who was the security officer. Tall, blond, beautiful, sexy and tough, ready for a fight. Well, remember they had Zena on the show?"

"Zena the Breast Warrior?" I say.

"Precisely," Mick says. "You look like her, not the blond."

I see Tit coming through the crowd. He has seen Mick and is making his way to us. The room is so full that he has to wedge his way between bodies. Mostly female bodies, so his journey is full of interruptions. But he makes it and looks at Mick.

"Hi, I'm Wade." He extends his hand, maintaining eye contact, softening Mick with his stare like he's attempting to hypnotize him. Then he turns to me, or rather looks up to me and lets his gaze fall gradually as if he needs to adjust focus with every change in contour and elevation. I reach to his chin and lift his eyes to mine.

"You know what I want to do, Wade?" I say to him. "Tit, they call you, don't they?"

"Yes," he says.

I grip his chin between my thumb and index finger. I see his eyes widen. I am strong, surprisingly strong. I feel anger. It's irrational anger. But it's there.

"I want to get you inside me and squeeze you until you come off and—"

Mick steps between us, breaking my grip on Tit's chin.

"This is my friend Ronnie," Mick says.

"Oh, hello," Tit says and backs into the crowd of people dancing. Someone has put on the Some Girls album and Miss You is cranked.

"This could be fun," I say to Mick, moving my hips and chest to the bass line.

"Well, it was a good strategy for scaring Tit away." He emphasizes Tit like it is a foreign word, spitting the word through his teeth. "And everyone watched it and everyone here is afraid of you except for him." He points to Moose, sitting on the bench along the barn-board wainscoting with his back to the red velvet wallpaper. He's looking at me and I'm looking at him and for a brief moment I'm looking at him and he's looking at me and then we're back in ourselves.

"Brilliant," Mick says from beside me. "Now he's really freaking out. Go and sit beside him."

I go and squeeze between him and another girl who is also on the bench. She's not with him. She's oblivious to him because she has her back to him and is talking to another girl on a chair.

"Excuse me," I say in my husky Zena the Breast Warrior voice.

"Fuck off, bitch," the girl says to me as I push in beside her. "There's no room."

"Well, I will make some," I say with all the wit and charm I can muster. I take her arm and throw her across the room where she is caught by a group of people who begin to protest with their "what the fucks." I ignore them and sit beside Moose. He is laughing, shaking and laughing.

"That was the best," he says to me. "Just the best."

"Thank you," I say. "Do you prefer her to me?" I look at my legs. Nice legs, I say to myself. It seems I have cut-off jeans and a white T-shirt with the Stones tongue and lips logo on the front in red. I have a huge bust. I lift them with my hands and push them up and down for Jagger who is watching.

"Not a chance," Moose says with a smile. "But I can't really see you very well. When you were over there I could see your face. But when you're close to me your head turns into a glowing ball."

"No way," I say, but I remember this completely.

"Oh yeah," Moose says, pointing a hand. "I can only make out faces from the other side of the room. As people get closer their head changes to a glowing ball. And you know the weird thing?"

"What?" I ask with mock innocence.

"The ball is two dimensional, not three. It's flat like a pancake and with fuzzy noise like a TV that's gone off the air."

"Oh," I say, looking at Mick and shrugging my shoulders.

"And that girl you came with."

"Yes?" I say again, wondering what is to come.

"Her face keeps changing to the face of Mick Jagger. That is too weird."

I put my hand on his leg. It's muscular and hard. Wow, I think. I bow close to him and he bows too so our faces are close.

"Listen," I say. "You're between worlds right now. Mescaline can do that."

"How do you know I'm on mesc?" he says, pushing my hand away. I take his hand in mine and look into his face.

"Because Mick and I are from between worlds. We are your guardian angels."

"Oh fuck," he says. I feel his palms sweat. His grip goes limp.

"Am I dying?" he says loudly between songs and everyone looks at us. I look at Mick and he throws his nose toward the door.

"C'mon, sweetie," I say. "Time to go."

He rises and stumbles and gets up again. People part to opposite sides of the room, opening our path to the door. We make it up the stairs, me supporting him and Mick holding the doors. The night air is cool and the cedar hedge adds a sweet green tinge to the breeze. Mick walks around the house and out onto the street. We follow and stop under a streetlight. I watch Mick shimmer and resolve into his old self. I feel shivers and realize that I too am a male again.

"That was fun," I say. "I would like to try that again soon."

"You mean become a girl?" Jagger says.

"Yeah."

"Next lifetime," he says. "It's too late for this one. You're dead."

He starts to laugh but then looks at me.

"I take that back. This is your last round, Ronnie." He looks at the asphalt and kicks a pebble. He looks up and says, "But no loss. You've been female before."

His words lie on the air like duff from a tree. I should be sad. I should not want to leave the earth experience. But I feel a desire. It must be something like a woman feeling the need to give birth. I look up and Jagger is studying me.

"I know, Ronnie. It's coming, the time, the event."

"What will it be like?" I ask him.

He shrugs his shoulders under his suit jacket. "I don't know, Ronnie. We've never done this one before."

"It's like that old Tom Waits song," I say, "Looking for the Heart of Saturday Night."

Jagger smiles with his eyes and a broad grin. "I would say it must be like that," he says.

"Who the fuck are you guys?" Moose says, startling us back to his presence.

36

Moose stands quietly off to the side in the castoff street lighting.

"I'm scared," he says. "This is too much."

"What are you seeing now?" Mick asks him.

"Dinosaurs," he says in a whiney kid voice.

Mick nods toward him, indicating him to me.

"He's between worlds?" I ask.

Mick nods and indicates him again with his nose raised. I walk over and pound Moose in the back with the base of my fist. He stands quietly, giving no indication that he knows he was hit or who it was that hit him. And then he looks around, up and down the street.

"He can't see us anymore," Mick says.

"Hey, Moose," I holler, but there's no response.

"He's back in his own world now," Mick says.

"What do we do? He's clearly still fucked up out of his head."

"Remember," Mick says calmly.

"Huh?" I say and look at Mick and then at Moose.

"I remember I heard a voice," I say. "I was standing here and I heard a voice speak but no one was around."

"What did the voice ask?" Mick says with a calm stance and voice.

"It didn't ask. It told. It told me to go home."

"Then tell him." Mick gestures with an open palm.

"He can't hear me."

"Look at the streetlamp," Mick says. "Become the light. Let your body settle into the same rhythm as that light."

I look up and watch. I stand in the light and I watch the light. I become so calm. I am as calm as the universe.

"What do I do?" Moose asks. He is looking at me.

"Go home," I say.

"But my old man is still up," he answers.

"Still, go home," I say.

He responds by turning and trudging up the small incline of the street like it's a mountain.

Mick walks up beside me and we follow together.

"This will be heavy," Mick says.

"I remember," I answer.

"No, you don't, because you never saw what we are about to see."

"Okay," I say and continue to walk slowly behind Moose. The parents' house is only a block away but it seems an interminably long journey. We cross at the crosswalk where Mick and I saw the flyer just a short while ago. Moose crosses, we follow.

He stops on the wood deck and looks around. He enters the porch and we follow. Mick closes the door behind us and looks at me, shaking his head.

"As if this makes any sense," he says.

The house is dark with only the blue-hue flashes of the TV off the walls and curtains. The volume is down low so the noise is more like mumbles. Our father is in his chair, a big-armed antique Mom got from her parents. His glasses are filled with reflections. He looks alien, unmoving, a character from another time.

"Dad," we hear Moose say.

"Yes, son," the gruff voice answers.

"I need you to stay up with me for a while."

"Why? Is something wrong?" The head does not move but continues to absorb the TV images.

"I did some drugs and I'm hallucinating. I'm afraid I might get hurt."

"Did you want to go to the hospital?"

"No, I'll be all right. I'll be coming down soon."

"Okay, son."

We watch Moose go over and sit and then lie down and then roll over and face into the back of the sofa. The sofa is large and of the same vintage as the chair Dad sits up from. We watch our father go over and pat his son's back and then go back and sit in his chair. The TV is a strobe and soft music is playing on a variety show. The room closes around us. Mick and I lean on the walls of opposite corners.

"Who's that?" I say. A figure has appeared beside our father and has its hand on his back. The figure changes colours, from red to yellow to orange.

"Remember, that's what I had you do to your Moose in the field," Mick says. "It's the release of the energy of the emotions. If that being was not present, doing what he's doing, your father would freak out. His emotions of this event would overwhelm him and his heart would fail."

"What emotions are being released?" I ask him. Mick just shakes his head and stands up straight, rubbing his elbow with his hand.

"We can guess. Remorse, failure, love, grief, all to do with seeing his son in a state he despises. It's a big lesson, Ronnie. What you despise and judge comes to you. And when it does, oh baby, it has a sting."

Our father gets up and disappears down the hall. He's a solid-backed man with a cowboy walk. I notice it. I notice everything, his belt and how low his pants hang, the muscle shirt he always wears, thin cotton and always white, clean. Watching him brings memories and the memories turn to visions.

I see him hitting fly balls to me and my friends in the back lot. I see our ten-year-old faces and sun-bleached hair. I see him cracking the balls off the bat in perfect arcs of motion and us first calling and then running and catching with our gloves. I see him at Park's Creek with a long-haired fifteen-year-old me, casting a line and the rod bending as a pike pulls the lure upstream. I see us later at a table and the Rapala filleting knife, long and pointed in his hand, and newspapers and fish guts as he pulls the skin taught to slice the flesh away. I see him and me with shredded clouds and a fall sky and shotguns over our shoulders, walking the damp woods.

I am shocked out of my daydreams. Light is blasting down the hallway from the parents' bedroom.

Moose

"What the hell," I say to Mick. But he doesn't respond because my mom is walking toward the living room. She has a blue housecoat and bare feet and black Irish hair. The three robed women accompanying her are the source of the light. She walks beside him, our Moose, lying with his face hidden. She puts her hands on him and presses her face to the back of his neck. She is speaking but I can only hear voice and not words. The women stand on each side behind her. They stand through the couch, through the walls. They stand inside things as if it was this room that lacked substance and not them. Lights flash like strobes or arc welders operating in darkness.

"She feels everything, your mum," Mick says, standing close to me. "It is her feelings being released by the others. That is what is freeing him, or you, or us." Mick smiles. His face is older now, the wrinkles more pronounced. He is leaning on my shoulder with his two crossed arms and his chin.

"This is big, Ronnie. You have no idea how big this is."

"It's like a dream, like a painting I knew: angels at the feet and head of Jesus while the Madonna looks on with a pierced heart. I've seen it before. It's so big. Mary's suffering is a key. Remember that Alice Cooper song, Only Women Bleed?"

Jagger looks at me. "I remember it through you. But it's true. Women possess a capability to suffer that is beyond men. It turns us into aliens by comparison. It's a mystery, Ronnie. Everyone thinks it was the suffering of Christ, but it was the suffering of Mary that brought the angels."

"McCartney wrote Let It Be after he had a dream about his mom whose name was Mary," I say absentmindedly. "She died when he was fourteen."

"Do you think she was helping him like your mum is helping you? I think so. The song was too immortal, even for McCartney. The Marys of the world are uniquely called as ministers, Ronnie. We are fortunate to have a Mary as our mum."

I nod. The three women and our mother lift themselves up. Mom wipes her face while the others dissipate into the dark.

"Were they praying?" I ask as our mother leaves down the hall.

"Yes, Ronnie. They were."

"Does prayer work then?"

"That kind does."

"What now?" I ask him.

"The parents are in bed. The others have left. This work is done for now."

"And what about us?" I ask.

"We can go. This was the big change. The turning point."

Moose is snoring in his contentment, a loud haul of air through snot. I look at him and then at Mick.

"But what do dead people do when they're not helping live people?" My voice is tight. And I feel fear, like something has come to an end.

"You wait around until they need you again," Mick says.

"When's that?"

"You'll know," Mick says. "Relax, you'll know."

Moose

We walk outside and back across the street to stand at the crosswalk. I turn to Mick and ask, "So what are we? Those helpers the parents had were like angels, but you and I, we're not angels."

Mick chuckles his *heh heh heh* laugh.

"Well, Ronnie, you know what Rilke said."

"Yeah, I do know what Rilke said. He said I am afraid that if I lose my demons my angels will take flight as well."

"It's perfect. Perfectly paradoxical," Mick says.

"So are we the demons?"

"You could say that," Mick answers with the austerity of a Lucifer. "The angel and demon thing is cooked up, but if there were ever demons we are them."

I nod to his statement and he continues.

"We are the engines of reality, Ronnie, to go where no one wants to go. We are the James T. Kirks of the starships. We stick our noses into other people's business. And because of us nothing is static." He begins to walk with long quick strides. I follow, hurrying to keep up.

"Even the flyers are necessary, Ronnie. Because it has to keep moving. Everything must be agitated to expand. The others, the glory beings, think we are a pain in their asses. But without us they're like tea drinkers. We give them a job. The Vietnam War created Thich Nhat Hanh."

Jagger stops, causing me to bump into him.

"You get it?"

"Yes."

"Good," and he starts marching again. We are heading toward the lake. We are on top of the 401 Bridge. The east begins to lighten. We are under the train trestle. We are rising the hill to Legresly's farm. The sky is lighting to our left. I smell the fishy smell of the lake. The marsh is on our right, the wind is up and I can see the lake, grey in the distance. We walk under chestnut trees and kick the prickly shells. We are at the beach. The whitecaps foam the surface of the water that rolls and heaves upon itself. The sky is morning pink and blue.

Mick stops and looks out over the lake. I stand with him and watch the quick-moving clouds.

"I must leave you, Ronnie," he says without looking at me.

"Why?" I ask like a child.

"Because I have nothing else to show you."

"Why?" I ask again. I feel weak so I sit down in the sand and gravel of the beach. I pick up a smooth stone the size of my palm and gently hold it.

"Because what you are no one understands, not even me."

"Will I have another guide?" I am looking at the stone in my hand, at the water that spreads at my feet.

"Possibly, but I don't know, Ronnie. I don't know."

"Don't leave," I ask, but no one answers, and when I look up I realize I am alone.

37

"Is this a dream?" I yell out, but there is no one listening. There is only the mighty hush of the surf.

And I stand alone. I've not felt dead until now. All the time with Jagger I never felt death but now it is upon me. I think I see a flyer close by and I turn and look. Even a galactic inter-dimensional emotion-harvesting alien would be a comfort and a companion right now. But I doubt that I have the energy to see one without Mick here, even if it were jumping on my head.

I know where I am. The graveyard where my dad is buried is a short walk. He must be dead if I am thinking he's dead. I have no idea if my life has passed or if I am still at some point along the way. I do remember it wasn't long after the party at Tit's that I met Aranka, my wife. We stayed married for a long time. I know that. But I only remember up until I left. It had been thirty-four years at that point. We had adopted a kid early on because we couldn't have any of our own. The kid had been taken away from her mother at three by children's aid. At that time I had only met the kid once. Her name is Lindsay and we were at a family reunion. She was skinny and had frizzed hair. Her eyes were brown and wide like doll eyes. And I carried her on my shoulders for walks and watched her run with the dogs.

The phone call came from my mom. Mom with the angels, Mom who understood life is a task, a journey, a place to do the right thing. She often regretted her decisions afterwards because life is also hard and takes nerves and resolve. And she hated to see anyone suffer.

But she called. We rambled on about nothing. Then she said, "They are putting Lindsay back into foster care."

"Hasn't that kid had enough of being passed around?" I asked. And then I had a brilliant idea. "You know what, Mom? We will adopt that kid." Lindsay was seven. We were her fifth home.

And she ran away at seventeen with a coke dealer. Then she came back one day with a black guy with long dreadlocks and showed us hand-knitted baby socks. And a while later we had a grandson. And the shit never stopped. But that kid became like a son. I taught him to ride a bike. Aranka taught him to read. He was six when I left, when I started this stupid time travel journey. And as far as I can figure, everything I have described is still future.

But here is a story. When my wife was young, about seventeen (she was twenty-nine when I met her) she was giving a rich kid horse-riding lessons. The father of the rich kid, the rich guy, offered to drive her home. On the way they chatted and he asked her what she was going to do with her life. And she answered, "One day I will adopt a seven-year-old girl that nobody wants." I found that out after the fact, after taking in the stray waif, after being married for seven years. Now that is destiny, or if not there must be someone like me, another Aranka, maybe a dead Aranka, following her around, steering her here and there, telepathically telling her what is going to happen.

And maybe that's what I need to do. The fucking dick Moose hasn't met Aranka yet. And sure as shit he'll fuck it up. I remember I almost hooked up with a speed freak. That's when Aranka and I met, she saved me. I need to guide him to her. It wasn't long after the experience with the mescaline that I met her. I need to be there and somehow get that dumbass to choose her. That is his and my destiny.

Boy, am I fucked up. I should walk up to Dad's grave. There's a nice tombstone. I remember his last words to me when he was sick, when he was all swollen and practically blind. "I hope my dad was proud of me." I wanted to say to him hold it, your dad was an asshole. But now I think I'm the asshole. I remember Dad, the way he would look at me with a faraway stare when I was young and doing dope. Like he was saying, How could that be my son? He never got me into the Motors. He worked at GM. Everyone worked at GM. It was easy street, good money, pension, benefits, out in thirty years. All my friends worked there, all my family worked there. It is true that a previous employer blackballed me, but still, my grandfather was vice president of the CAW. I remember telling Aranka, Dad never got me to the Motors because he was ashamed of me.

"No way," she answered. "That's not fair to say that."
"It is true," I answered her. It was true, I say now.
Should I feel better after spilling all this? I don't know.

A car pulls up. I wait and watch. A white guy about forty gets out and goes to the back door and reaches in. I know he is unbuckling a kid. And then a little boy in a white T-shirt and blue shorts and crocs runs around the car. He looks my way but obviously doesn't see me. I wave but he does not respond. I call out to the dad, "Good morning." But he walks on toward the beach. I am invisible again. And that kid has me thinking about my grandson.

"Grumpa," he called me. We would jump on the trampoline together. A big loaf of a middle-aged guy and a little black kid, laughing and shouting and wrestling. And riding bikes down the trails by our home in Sunderland. And at the skate park, him on his scooter. Wipeouts and cuts and tears and me, sometimes angry, sometimes harsh, just like the old man. So many times I said, I have become him. And then the memories flood and I have no emotion but love.

And that surprises me because all my anger and all my blame have turned into something else. If I have learned anything from being dead it's that you look at your life and you want it, all of it. I remember a Mel Gibson film and it begins with a kid jumping off a roof, and on the way down he realizes everything was perfect. And you see, I am now beginning to realize I will never get back to my life. It is another me who will live what I only remember. And that thought leaves me hollow and empty. He will get married and adopt that kid and help raise that grandson and have that long marriage. I can only help him to not fuck it up. I can only help him to realize what is precious. I can help him to stave off his irrational ideas and beliefs before he really hurts himself or someone. I need to keep him from his self-indulgence, his feeling sorry for himself. Because when you feel sorry for yourself you do stupid shit. I think I can do that. I think I can do that. It is a noble endeavour. And then I will see what happens with me.

38

I start to walk. The old cottages along the beach are all dark. The moon is still up but the silver slice of light is fading against the dawn. I walk slower. Past homes I knew. Past the lives of people I knew.

The Duetta's, a rendezvous house for me and Dewy, Caz and Hans, always hanging out there. Old Garney, Dewy's dad, who fixed up the old red Pontiac with black bucket seats and a floor shift and then Dewy totalled it at Harmony Road and King Street in Oshawa. We were on our way to the movies and the light turned yellow.

"We'll never make it to the fucking movie," Caz said from the front.

"Oh yes we will," Dewy said and tramped it and pulled to the inside lane around the stopped traffic and into the front corner of a big new Oldsmobile that was making a left turn. We were all knocked out cold. Later we were told they had to pull the cars apart with two tow trucks. No one was seriously hurt. Those old cars were like tanks. But Dewy had some cracked ribs and Caz had some cuts on his face.

Moose

I look at the old house now, just a tiny place but full of life. Cars are parked everywhere around the large yard, all in various states of repair and disuse. Some have grass growing up around them. Some have no hoods or doors.

I remember the crunch of steel and standing at the corner. They had taken Dewy and Caz off in an ambulance. I was standing there and a girl came and asked if I was okay. And she asked me to come to her house so I could call my dad. And I remember Dad came to the girl's home to pick me up. He came in the house and the mother greeted him. It was a house of girls. There were girls and women everywhere and the girl's mom offered him a coffee which he politely declined. I was sitting at the table, shaken up. The girl who had brought me back was sitting beside me. Long straight hair and a muscle shirt with a stretchy body thing that covered her from above the breasts to below. The muscle shirt was oversized and billowy. And she had on tight jeans and runners with no socks. I can picture her so well, and the large kitchen with the mom talking to dad. She was a good-looking woman too, with short permed hair and a T-shirt and jeans. And she had bare feet.

Why am I remembering this?

And I picture Dad so calm. And when he motioned for me to come, he was so calm. I had expected him to be upset and anxious but instead he was calm. I had expected him to be, "Thank god you're alive," but instead he was detached and distant. It was a resignation. It was like he was accepting that what he had hoped would not happen was happening. Like what his life had taught him was inevitable, and what he had tried to prove was not inevitable was in fact inevitable. His son was going to get in trouble and get hurt and life would be life, as it always had been.

And as I walk I think of my own grandson, my daughter, and all the hell I had lived through when I departed. I was always wanting to make things different, to sidestep the grief and the anxiety. I wanted everyone to cooperate in my dream of life where suffering and pain had ended and we could just have fun and enjoy peace and harmony forever.

I laugh.

The world is waking up. I hear voices and dishes and smell cooking, eggs and toast. Cars pass me on the road. The people come out of houses. I see Mr. Duetta, Old Garney, come out and get in one of the cars. It starts and belches a gasp of exhaust and then backs out the driveway like a derby car, swinging sideways on the road and then accelerating in a rush of splattering engine noise. I sit down on the edge of the asphalt with my feet stretching into the ditch. Every now and then I crane my neck to see people come out of the cottages. People dressed nicely, all going off to jobs. I figure the cottages are now homes. I see a nicely dressed woman in a dress and blouse get into a nice Oldsmobile. I remember I know her from somewhere but can't remember where. I look into the ditch and watch the insects that collect on the goldenrod and the Queen Anne's lace, and the bluebells at the side of the road. Colours of white and yellow and blue in a row like a mini hedge of beauty. I stoop closely to watch bees and mini bees, flies and mini flies and white-winged butterflies land and lift off from the flowers. I sit. The wind moves the trees and I look up at the beauty of leaves, tall maple trees that disperse sunlight and the diamonds of brilliance through holes in the canopy. I follow the leaves to branch to trunk and observe the thick bark that layers like a skin, grey wood that raises in patterns of age. The ditch beside me is black with decaying deposits of this tree. And its roots drink its own self.

The metaphor is not lost on me.

The sky has dimmed. People are returning. Kids on buses, getting out of the bifold doors. Red lights flashing. People return to their homes. I turn to look at the Duetta's once more but the house is gone. And I remember it that way also. When I was married and I came back here. The house was gone and the yard a vacant lot. I sit. I am disoriented. I don't know time or year. I have been sitting here and nothing has changed, but everything has changed. I sit until the night comes. I get up and begin to walk.

I walk toward the graveyard. I remember Dusty's funeral. Me and Ted and Oscar. Ted was my best man. He tried to stay in touch. I never reciprocated. Why? Because I am an asshole. But once we adopted our daughter, I never had time. I was always living in overwhelm. She loved horses so we bought her one. And then the horse shows and the barn and the coaches and the bullshit. Because she never got along with anyone. Years later I understood. My daughter had faced challenges no one I have ever met has faced. I once told a social worker if an adult had received the treatment my daughter had received as a three year old, they would call it torture. She didn't trust people. She couldn't. Once I figured it out it all made sense. And once I figured it out, I could love her. I could give her a break. Even after family court over the grandson and my liver spewing toxic enzymes for months, I figured it out. Fuck.

The sky has darkened and the stars are appearing. The breeze is quiet. The smells of weeds, sweet and stringent, like fly spray and honey, rise as if they were released. Abandoned fields, noxious weeds, spreading in the human disconcern. Darkening with the slow-turning planet. Fading as I fear I am fading.

I worked for the same boss for twenty-five years. We met at church and became friends. After I was at the job for six years he left for England for six months of missionary training. He left after Christmas and put me in charge. In January the temperatures dropped to minus twenty and stayed there for thirty days. We were a heating company that delivered heating oil. We had a bulk plant where we stored oil and where other companies would load. I put on thirty pounds and killed my diesel-powered Jetta.

He came back and after a few years had a nervous breakdown. Again, I was asked to run the show. This time by his father. "Do me a favour, take on a few extra responsibilities for a while." I said that I would be glad to do whatever was required. Which I did.

A few years later he gave half his company to a friend from church.

The new partner had a heart attack. Again, I ran the company. When I left my life, he had put me on the road in sales. I was doing pretty good and making decent money. But he had made his sister general manager and he was grooming his son to take over the company. I was on the outs. I had always hoped to have stakes in the game, to have a partnership. But I was running sales calls to make my living. Never-ending fucking sales calls. Fuck.

I am at the cemetery. I walk in the gate, black steel lacquered thick and shiny. The hinges creak and squeak. It seems to disturb something. The road lifts up the hill. Flowerbeds fill spots here and there.

I was drinking a lot and had started smoking pot again when I left. Holsten German beer, 7.8 percent alcohol by volume, dark, rich and bitter and a little sweet. It was an addiction. I could punch those things down. And I would sit and think. Stew, Mom called it when Dad would do it. "Your father would stew over things," she would say.

Sometimes I would clean up, do the energy thing. That's where I was when I started this journey. I was cleaning up. Getting on a new track. Hell of a lot of good it did me. But it was a good distraction. I needed a distraction. My love for my grandson was killing me. Because I had no power, no authority in his life. I was doing all kinds of stuff to support him. He was with us a lot, because we wanted to save him from hazard. Both parents were fighting for custody. Police and SWAT and accusations and in the middle of it all a little boy we had grown to love as much as our own lives.

So we took him, Danicko, as much as we could.

Here we were, myself past middle age and my wife a senior. We had horses. We had a bit of money. But I always had a guilt trip that I wasn't doing enough for that kid. I would watch him try so hard to be a good little boy but he could not.

No wonder I'm dead.

I have to lie down. I haven't slept since I was killed. But now I'm tired.

39

I sit and then lay back. The ground is hard and the grass is wet. I close my eyes. I hear steps on the gravel path. I open my eyes. My father stands looking down at me. And I don't know who I am or where I am when I say, "Oh. Hi Dad."

"Hi Butch." He always called me that. I had forgotten.

I get to my feet, losing my balance and regaining it.

"I like the tombstone," he says.

I turn. There it is. I never realized this was where I had stopped walking. The stone is polished a glazed black. There is a light from the moon so I can see the inscriptions.

MILTON RONALD POTTER, 1938–2004, and the scripture from Job: I KNOW THAT MY REDEEMER LIVES, AND THAT I WILL SEE HIM WITH THIS BODY, WITH THESE EYES UPON THE EARTH. And there's a fish, a trout jumping out of the water with a fisherman with a rod and line, the fish arching for freedom. The stone has a small garden around it with some geraniums. Mom's tending.

I close my eyes. I saw him. I'm certain of that. But I am dead and probably delusional. I mean, I've been hanging out with Mick Jagger. How could this be my father? I can smell cigarette smoke. He is just waiting. He was always good at waiting.

"Hi Dad. How's it going?"

My eyes are closed.

"I'm fine, son. How are you?"

It's his voice, for sure. I remember C.S. Lewis talking about loved ones who had died. He said when you forget their voice, you've forgotten them. But I always remembered Dad's voice.

"Open your eyes," he says. His voice is kind like he's talking to a child.

I do. He stands behind the tombstone. I remember seeing pictures of him when he married Mom. He was 130 pounds with thick Buddy Holly glasses and sideburns. He was tough. His life had been hell with my grandfather. He grew lean, like a beanpole with fists of gravel. That's who he is now as he stands before me. He's like a James Dean caricature or maybe James Dean was a caricature of him. A cigarette with a burning ember hangs out of the side of his mouth. He removes it with his two forefingers, the ones I remember being nicotine stained all his life. He removes it and says, "How are you, Butch?"

"I never imagined you'd be here," I say.

"Well, it kind of makes sense," he says. "You came here for something. It may have been to meet me."

I look around. "Are other dead people here?"

"No." He shakes his head and tosses the cigarette and stomps it with a boot. "No one comes here anymore."

"They used to?" I ask.

"Oh yeah. But not now. Things are changing. The dead don't think of themselves as being dead anymore. They can build and move around. These old places are boring to them. Or us, I should say."

"I've missed you," I say.

He shakes his head. "No you haven't. I've been with you all along."

"I never knew it."

"You did," Dad answers.

I shrug my shoulders. "Doesn't sound like this is going to be sentimental."

Dad laughs. His face becomes almost Oriental. His great-grandmother was a full-blooded Indian so it makes sense. His cheeks wrinkle and his forehead collapses and his eyes squint and his mouth brims wide with cheer. I start laughing with him.

"That was funny," he says. "So like you to be the philosopher. We have a job to do and we need to do it sooner than later."

"What job is that?" I ask.

"Steering your living soul to his destiny."

"I've done some of that already," I say with a chuckle.

"We all have," Dad says.

"Dad. Am I really dead?"

He smiles and looks at me. "There's no such thing."

So what am I? I am separate from myself. I am not a part of him anymore. I can talk to him and help him but I am not him. Am I the part of him that fucked up? Am I the fuckup version in some parallel universe?

"No, it's not like that," Dad answers. "It's nothing like that."

"Then I have no idea."

"It's strange," Dad says with a smirk. "Really weird."

"Tell me then," I say.

"I don't think you can handle it."

"I'm dead. What's to handle?"

"I overheard everything you were saying back there. The story of how it never worked the way you wanted. The job, the family, the marriage."

"That's how I felt when I was alive. I felt like I just couldn't measure up. Like I should have done better." I cross my arms and go over and sit my ass on the tombstone.

"Well, there's a secret, you know," he says, lifting his mouth into a half smile.

"Okay," I say. "Lay it on me."

He pauses and takes out a pack of smokes, taps one out and puts it in his mouth. Takes out some matches, strikes one and lifts it to his face, illuminating his features and lighting his cigarette. He shakes out the match and tosses it to the ground. Inhales on the burning stick and with a lung full of smoke says, "You are the creator of them all."

"What?" I say under a breath.

"Out of your beliefs, out of your expectations, out of what you wanted to experience, came all the people in your life." He taps an ash to the ground and watches it fall, shuffling a foot and laughing.

"No way," I say.

"You know, son, a moment ago nothing existed and a moment ago nothing existed and a moment ago nothing existed. Everything happens instantly, and when it happens we humans miraculously create a story to support it. The story didn't create the happening, the happening created the story." He laughs again.

"I can't get my head around that," I say, pressing my hands against the hard edge of the stone for reassurance.

"Nobody can get their head around it because their head is part of what is being created and it comes with its own story." Dad is smiling like he's the cat who caught the bird.

"No. No, no, no, no, no," I say, raising my hands to grip my head.

"It doesn't matter," he says, grabbing my one hand with his own and moving it away from my face. He looks into my eyes, stooping. "It doesn't matter." His voice is soft and low. "The only thing that matters is that you understand who they are."

I lower my hands to my lap and look at him.

"Because," he says, "if you understand who they are you will love them as yourself." He slows the words at the end.

"Ever heard the saying love your neighbour as yourself?"

I nod. Several times.

"How do you feel about all the people in your life now? How do you feel about how you were treated? How do you feel about the assholes? All the things that really upset you, that really pissed you off about people, you gave them those traits. You gave them those lives. You gave them the positions in your life. It's all so you could become more."

"More what?" I say, looking up at him.

"More perfect," Dad says. "More developed, like a tree that gets pruned. We use life after life after life to prune ourselves into a person we never imagined we would be."

"That doesn't seem fair," I say. "And what of the ones I created? What do they become?"

"They do the same," Dad says. "It never ends. It's how you began. It's how I began. We were ideas from someone else, from their ideas and feelings and beliefs. And it goes on and on, never ending."

"It's a bit overwhelming," I say, getting to my feet.

"But it's so easy," Dad says. "Every being charts their own course. Once we begin we never stop. And we just need to accept and love. That's the easiest thing in the universe. But you need to accept and love yourself, son. You have to understand that they don't feel what you feel. The more lifetimes we live the more sensitive we get. It goes with the territory. The newer ones don't feel it. Don't expect them to."

"Right." I say. "They are numbskulls."

We both laugh at the Bugs Bunny idiom, culled from our shared heritage of sarcasm and wit.

"I will tell you something," Dad says. "When you accept and love your creations, it is impossible to hate yourself. You can't do it because you are part of the same soul as them. It's when you're hard on yourself that you are hardest on others."

"If it's so easy, why didn't I get it sooner? Like why go through all the shit?" I say it like I'm mad but I'm not. Listening to him has made me soft.

"You need to grow to the place where you can accept ideas. It's stuff you arrive at. It's like a journey to places and the places are where you think of yourself in a new way. The new thing is always an idea. The universe is made up of ideas. You've come a long way." He smiles and cuffs a hand behind my neck.

"C'mon. I've got something to show you."

40

"What's that?" I say.

"Did you see the truck?"

I look to the road allowance that runs alongside the fence. I dimly see a pickup. I walk toward it.

"It's your old pickup," Dad says.

"1979 Chev with the 350 truck engine, four by four with bucket seats," I say and turn to Dad. "You brought that? I pulled a plow with that truck. I welded so many ties and braids to keep it together that the wind caused it to hum."

Dad nods and lifts the burning coal to his face. It glows as he inhales.

"Keys are in it," he says.

"Are you coming?"

"Oh yeah," he answers. "I want to see this."

We walk over to the truck parked in the shadow of a lone streetlamp on the graveyard drive. The body is brown and full of rust scab. Sections of the rocker panels are missing. I get in and Dad gets in on the other side. I find the keys in the ashtray. The cab rocks with the engine turning over.

"Once I was driving this and the starter engaged. I had to pull over and the engine was struggling against the slower revs of the flywheel. I got out and lifted the battery connection off and the engine stalled. Then I put the clamp back on the pole, got in and turned the key and the engine started. No damage to the starter or the flywheel."

Dad is laughing at the story. "They made them tough back then."

The engine starts and I push the clutch and drop the shift into first. It's metal on metal with a clink when the gears mesh. I pull out onto the gravel road and accelerate, shifting through the gears.

"Heavy metal, man. Where to, Dad?"

"The Oshawa Auto Auction," he says.

I laugh and slap the steering wheel. "What are we doing there?"

"We are introducing him to her," he answers.

"But that happens anyway," I say.

"Not without us."

"But you never even liked her," I say, leaning on the wheel and looking sideways at him.

"I liked her just fine. But I was worried. She was ten years older than you. You were only a kid."

"Do you know what happened to me, this me?" I say, gripping my T-shirt in a fist and pulling it toward him.

"That's why I'm here," he says. "We want to get this right. She is his destiny. And guess what?"

"What?" I answer. But before he answers back I say, "I'm tired of that guy. It drains me to be around him."

"This is it," Dad says. "You are free after this."

"And why is that?" I ask. My thoughts have slowed and so has the truck.

"Because she is your creation. You created her to look after him. Her energy and her tenacity will pull him though. She will be a real pain in the ass at times. But he will make it."

"Make it where?" I say.

"To where you wanted him to go."

We are both quiet after that.

"What do mean I created her for him?"

Dad smiles. "Gotcha on that one. There is only one subconscious for all of you. And the subconscious reads all of you like a blob of questions and desires. But basically it memorizes everything you want to experience and then sends that out in every direction, to each personality, so you all live through each other."

I watch the road in the headlights. Trees and brush and lanes, then a rabbit darts into the headlights. It's a jackrabbit and it's big.

"Remember some of the hares you would shoot at the farm?" I ask him.

He smiles. "I tied one by the ears around my belt and it was still dragging its feet. That was the largest I've ever seen. Your mom made stew, and was it good."

"Mom can cook game," I say.

Dad grins.

"You loved the ducks," he says.

"Aranka hated them."

"But she ate them."

"She liked the teal," I say.

Dad nods. "Memories are heavy," he says. "They pull you down. Can you feel them? You tolerate them until you get to the ones you are to assist. I think they send the memories to attract you. Then you do your stuff and when you're done you leave the memories for good because you can. You fly away like a swallow, past the eagle and into your freedom.

"Kevin talked about the eagle and so did Mick Jagger. Now you talk about the eagle. If I remember, it eats awareness, and gruesomely."

"It takes a lot to get past the eagle."

"Did you say I will be free?"

"Yes, once he has Aranka he won't need you and you will be free."

I slow my thoughts and the truck and turn up Mill Street toward the 401.

"You created him," Dad says.

"No. I've been following him."

"No. You created him and her."

"That night I brought her home. You were so stubborn."

"Do you remember what was said?" Dad asks.

"Yes. I told you we were getting married and then you asked me if I wanted to know what you thought of that."

"And you said no." Dad laughs. His cigarette is burning the filter and it stinks like sour rubber.

"Throw out that thing, will ya?"

He cranks down the window and tosses the butt.

"And then you enumerated our differing ages over a forty-year span, decade by decade. When you're forty she'll be fifty. When you're fifty she'll be sixty. When you're sixty she'll be seventy." I shake my head but Dad laughs so hard he starts coughing and I laugh too.

He catches his breath. "You needed me. You needed someone to push off of. Every good parent plays that game for you. You needed it so you could become yourself."

A quiet pause fills the air between us.

"And you could never have survived the Motors."

I turn my head to look at him and then turn back to the road as we turn onto the 401 ramp.

"Your soul would have died. It was the best thing I ever did for you, not helping you get in. And that foreman at Courtice Steel that gave you the bad reference, you owe everything to him."

I don't answer.

"You know I'm right."

"Yes," I answer.

"And I was never ashamed of you. You were just so different. I had never imagined you would be so different."

"Different than what?" I say.

"Different than me," he says. "I wanted you to be a chip off the old block. But I never found the block you were chipped from. Until now."

"It makes sense," I say. "This whole trip of being dead has shown me that being alive is quite the big deal."

He horks a snot out the open window and looks over at me.

"No matter what you think of your life, son, you were always fired up. Something was always stirring. And that woman of yours was the one to keep you on your toes."

"I see what you're saying," I say.

"I was proud of you that you stood up to me and married her. You had to have balls to marry her. She never took a back seat to anyone and you needed to earn her respect."

"Which I did," I say.

"Yes. Yes, you did."

The cab quiets until the puffing noise of the leaking exhaust manifold is the only sound.

"Thanks, Dad," I say.

"For what?"

"For being proud of me."

"No problem, son."

"Was your father proud of you? I remember you had wanted him to be proud of you when you were sick."

"He was, son. And I was proud of him."

"Better be careful," I say. "This could turn into a real tearjerker."

"Seriously," he says. "He was the perfect father for me. He put the me in me."

"Just like you put much of the me in me," I say to him.

Dad laughs, a hearty wheezing laugh.

I pull off at Courtice Road and turn south and take the service road to the auction. The sun is coming up and I see lights in the garage. The doors are open and cars are moving out of the bays.

"Park here," Dad says.

I pull into a spot alongside the chain-link fence that surrounds the parking area. I turn off the engine. We wait.

"But if you really want to thank someone for your freedom, thank that daughter of yours."

"Did you want me to adopt her?"

"I was starting to get it. I knew that kid would push you into the next dimension of yourself. And she did. In the end your love for her was your final victory that will seal your success over the eagle. She was relentless and you needed someone like that to crack the skull of your resistance to the infinite."

"Then I was a hard skull to crack."

"Do you remember what you were like after you had the awakening?"

"Are you referring to my ability to move around, back and forth in my life? To change the past and future, to get killed and become a spirit being?"

"Yes, it was just prior to that. You were being called. That is what gave you the inspiration to do what you did, to become what you became."

"Yes. I was willing to experience anything for love. I was able to do amazing things that I always thought were beyond me. I had no cares and did so much. It was life at its peak and it lasted for thirty years. Or it will last for thirty years."

"You understood that they gave that to you, your wife, your daughter, your grandson, your boss, your parents." He smirked and scratched his ear. "What a gift. To be pushed out of yourself into the light of all beings, to sail past the eagle."

The sky is light at the rim of Lake Ontario to the east. The streetlights on the highway are still on. A green Nova passes us and turns into the entrance in front of us.

"It's them," I say. "What year is that Nova, Dad?"

"Looks like a '70 but I could be wrong. One last thing before we get into this."

"Yes?" I say.

"You did not ever want, in any way conceivable, to become a partner in that business. You know we, the dead, get to listen in on the thoughts of the living, and I heard you say it over and over, so many times, how you were mistreated and not given what you were worth. And every time, I said Jesus Christ, Ronnie, give it a break."

I fall to snickering because I know he is telling the truth.

"All you ever wanted was to make good money with as little responsibility as possible, so you could ride your horse, drink booze with your wife, write your poems and stories and hang out with that kid. That's all you wanted and those guys gave it to you."

"I know it's the truth, Dad."

"We all get what we ask for. You've been clear. Many aren't, so they get shit lives. You have a good one."

"Had," I say.

"No, have. It continues forever. And you are now getting what you asked for. You are detaching from your life like a balloon on a string. And you asked for that, son."

"Yeah, I know I did."

"Look," he says.

41

I smile. "Fuck, Dad," I say. "This is tough."

"I know, son. It's like a dream. It always is."

I watch the green Nova pull up to the doors. It stops and she gets out, my life partner, my left hand, my flesh as one. She is wearing blue overalls and her hair is shoulder-length blond under a blue jean bandana. She opens the trunk and hauls some garbage bags inside the building. Her mother, my mother-in-law, gets out with a cigarette dangling out of one side of her mouth. She has on the same blue overalls. Her hair is bundled up behind her head. She is wearing rubber boots. I remember them both in those overalls with rubber boots and yellow plastic gloves, washing the car interiors while I did the exteriors. Soaked to the ass all the time.

Dad is quiet beside me. He taps a smoke out of a pack and then bows his head when he lights it. The thin smell of tobacco fills the cab and disperses. The girls have gone inside. Trucks rumble up and down the 401. We watch them and alternatively turn and watch the grey building. Cars come and park. People get out and go inside. People going to their jobs, always living, always carrying the torch of being human.

I see a grey Pontiac Laurentian pull up. "It's the Rowleys," I say to Dad.

He just nods and watches.

"Dave introduced us."

He nods again. "He was a tool of destiny." Dad laughs.

"I should yell out, Hey, tool."

Dad smirks with a knuckle against his nose.

I hear before I see a car that huffs like a steam engine with white exhaust billowing.

"How long did you drive it like that?" Dad asks.

"Remember it died just after Aranka and I met. I think I set a record for driving with a blown head gasket."

"I think you did," Dad answers.

We watch the car turn in and park where the office staff park. The engine stops belching and he gets out. The first thing I notice is his long tangled hair and beard. He looks like some mountain hillbilly. A beer bottle falls out and lands on the asphalt and he stoops to pick it up and toss it back into the car. He stands up and stretches, arching backwards, and then walks toward the parking lot.

"I'm following him," I say to Dad. "Do you think I should?"

"Why not?" he says. "No one will recognize you."

"Yeah, that's right. I've done this before."

Dad nods again and covers his mouth with his cigarette-carrying hand. He exhales a lung of smoke and says, "Get goin'. What are you waiting for?"

I exit the truck and cross the lot from where we are parked. The bay doors are thirty feet tall and all of them are pulled up. It's a beautiful day. The sun is casting the parking lot in a huge shadow from the building. I go inside and look up at the tall ceiling and the hanging bell-shaped lights. People are walking in and out. Cars are being driven into the bays, forming lines of multicoloured tin with chrome mirrors and bumpers. A Dodge Dart, a Mustang, an Olds 442, a Rambler, yellow, green, orange, blue. I am standing, observing, dreaming, when I see him with the Rowleys, my younger self with his two friends. They see me watching them and I nod and walk away.

And then I see her, my future wife, and her mother. They are taking cleaning stuff from the corner to the benches beside the work area. I remembered Zena always looked young, but now I see her from this detached place and she is beautiful with her dark hair and her features which are dark like a Spanish person's. She doesn't look Czech at all. Her complexion is dark and her eyes are dark. Her blue overalls are tight-fitting and she has a good figure trapped in there.

"How can I help you?" she says when she notices me. Her words are foreign and it sounds like she chews English before she speaks it.

I step back like someone just hit me.

And then from behind me Aranka steps around and into my view.

"Can we help you?" she says in a soft clear voice. I look and she smiles at me with her head on a slight angle like she's in a hurry and needs an answer.

"Uh, uh," I stammer. I can't talk because everything is being used up in observation. I remember this so vividly and now I am living it. Her hair is blond and thin and falls out from under the blue bandana which has coloured opaque patches. Her mouth is wide and her eyes are blue and her cheeks are high. Her skin is pale and almost translucent. I look down and notice again that she has the same blue overalls as her mom but she's packed even tighter into hers.

Memories flood. How Rowley told me I should work for her and that she had a great ass and never wore a bra. I remember the sex and adopting Lindsay and the grandson Danicko, the houses, thirty acres in Claremont and Ayr and then Sunderland and the people who lived with us, Carol the stranger and Natasha the niece, and brother Rob and Chuck the schizophrenic, and Paul the criminal. I remember the horses we had, and the dogs and the cats. And I ride these memories like Thor on his Kon-Tiki raft until she interrupts me.

"Do I know you?" she says. Her face has dropped into a mild concern. She must have picked up on my emotional ride. She was always intuitive that way.

I muster my courage. I'm going to tell her the truth.

"You do," I say. "I'm from the future."

"Oh, well then," she answers with a smile. "At least that's better than the past."

I laugh. We both laugh.

"What's the future like?" she asks.

"It's good," I say. "Worthwhile, for sure. It's a big improvement on the past."

We are interrupted by a big-bearded haggard guy in a T-shirt that's torn at the armpit and jeans that have faded to a purple and Dash runners.

"Those are Chinese jeans," I say, but she doesn't hear me.

"I want a future different than my past," she says to me. I look at her but she is looking at him. I am looking at him. His eyes are lazy and he's smiling.

"He's stoned," I say.

He walks up and she extends her hand.

"You must be Ron," she says. "Dave Rowley said you were coming."

He takes her hand and gently shakes it.

"Yes," he says.

"I'm Aranka. Nice to meet you," she says, but he's looking at me.

"She's the one," I say to him.

"C'mon and I'll show you what to do," she says to him again.

He looks at her and then back at me and then at her.

She walks away and he follows, but reluctantly, like he's stuck to me with some ectoplasmic cosmic material. But he leaves and goes with her and I leave and walk outside to go back to the truck. But I stop and remember that I heard those words when Aranka shook my hand that first time. I remember a voice that said, "She's the one." If I hadn't heard that voice I may never have sealed the deal and gone with her.

She was ten years older than me and had many previous relationships, sexual relationships, and I was a virgin. A behemoth of a virgin, but still a virgin. She scared the hell out of me with stories of guys that were ridiculous idiots and how they treated her. I would never have had the guts to get involved but for the voice that said, "She's the one."

And it was me. I was the voice. A dead me who created a parallel life, who managed to arrive here and seal my own fate.

I am still standing there when the truck drives up. Dad is driving and he pulls up with the passenger door right in front of me.

"C'mon, son," he says. "We're done here. It's time to go."

I get in and he slowly releases the clutch, moving out of the parking lot and onto the service road and out the ramp onto the highway heading east.

And there are two suns and a giant mountain that rises black against the horizon, roughly shaped like the head of an eagle. I lose track of time because time has become an idea, not a fact, and the suns are constantly behind the mountain. And as we get closer I can see the mountain moves like a black jelly mould and there is an orange glow in its belly. I can see things flying to it, small dots like black holes that fly into the belly where the orange glow grows and diminishes like breathing.

"I guess you know what that thing is?" Dad says and I just nod. "And the other things? Are those the flyers?"

"Yeah. They feed the eagle. Nothing gets past the eagle unless it's purified."

As we drive we watch. The orbs enter the blackness like coal into a furnace. We approach a crowd of onlookers gathered on the edge of the highway. A man stands in the middle of the pavement and waves us over.

"I thought we could get by," he says. Perspiration is dripping from his chin. "They told us we could get by."

"Go back to your life," Dad tells him. "No shortcuts. If there is anything in you that the eagle can swallow, he'll swallow you with it."

"And what about you?" the man bellows.

"The eagle has no interest in us," Dad says and rolls up the window and drives past the man, past the crowd and past the massive darkness until the light of the two suns becomes all that we see.

"What do you make of those?" I ask.

"Some things are worthy of no comment, son. And some other things just cannot be commented upon."

CPSIA information can be obtained
at www.ICGtesting.com
Printed in the USA
BVHW081913281020
591951BV00001B/7